Under the Tamarisk Tree

FLORI PAQUETTE

ISBN: 979-8-89031-899-2 (sc)
ISBN: 979-8-89031-900-5 (hc)
ISBN: 979-8-89031-901-2 (e)

One Galleria Blvd., Suite 1900, Metairie, LA 70001
(504) 702-6708

CONTENTS

PROLOGUE

It has been over twenty years since we lived through the final chapters of this story. I still have dreams where, overcoming all opposition, I pick up the phone and call the police. When I awaken, the truth I can never change squeezes my heart.

CHAPTER 1

Days of Milk and Honey 1978

Our future was as bright as the sky was blue with dreams sweet like spring mountain air on that June day. Our families sat in folding chairs, and our friends were spread out on picnic blankets over the pine needles. Dan and I stood in the clearing at the forest's edge. We unrolled the parchment scroll containing our handwritten marriage vows and took our turns reading them to each other in front of our small gathering. Afterward, everyone celebrated with potluck hors d'oeuvres and champagne at my maid of honor's house.

We flew out from under our parents' wings and moved so Dan could finish school. He began his sophomore year in the fall. Our income was his student loan money, and I landed a job cooking in a downtown coffee shop. There wasn't much in our till, but we always paid our rent and never went to bed hungry.

I worked with a line cook and a waitress who seemed jazzed up about Jesus. They seemed to have a lot in common because they chatted about the church they were going to. I had always wanted to be close to God but didn't understand the church thing. My curiosity perked up. I listened in on what they had to say.

They seemed to be excited about a concert that was coming up on the weekend. They told me that the group was hot and gave me the time and place.

When I got home, I told Dan about it. "Honey, there are some people I work with who go to a church where a lot of college kids go. They make it sound fun. Would you be interested in checking it out?"

"Maybe."

"They told me about a Christian band that is playing this weekend."

"Hmm, really? Are you interested in going?"

"I'm kind of curious. My coworkers are pretty charged up about it. They don't seem like boring fuddy-duddies."

"Well, if you want to go, maybe we should see what it's like. We aren't doing anything else this weekend."

It was surprising to see so many enthusiastic young people at a Christian concert. I had expected something more subdued. The stage was set up like at a rock concert with drums, electric guitars, and electronic keyboards. When the band sauntered out on the scene, Dan and I looked wide-eyed at each other.

The music was terrific. It was not the kind about God I had ever heard before. We rocked along with everyone else as Jesus was presented to us in lyrics that spoke our kind of language.

After the band finished playing, the lead singer invited anyone who wanted a personal relationship with Jesus to raise their hand and go forward for prayer. Both Dan and I left our seats and went up by the stage.

That was when we met Barney. There were a lot of people around, but he took the time to congratulate us and pray with us. His first instructions were for us to read the Bible and find a Christian church to attend.

My coworkers invited us to visit their church. After listening to all they said, it sounded like a great place to start. It turned out that

Barney was the associate pastor there. I felt like a flower blooming in the morning sun.

We joined Barney's college-age Bible study. I loved to listen to him play his guitar and teach us worship songs. It was great to sit around and learn about Jesus with other people our age. We all became close friends.

Every Thursday morning, Barney would come over to our funky old apartment. We would drink coffee, eat my homemade muffins, and study the book of Romans in our crisp new Bibles. After we prayed, he'd be on his way before Dan's first class of the day.

Barney taught us about the meaning and necessity of baptism. Dan and I chose to hold hands as he submerged us together. It seemed like breathing in a new kind of air when we came up out of the water. Our time as newborns in the Lord couldn't have been sweeter or more nourishing.

My childhood dreams came true when I found out I was going to have a baby. I felt complete. Dan's face went red when I told him—I suppose from the shock of romance and reality crashing together. As a business major, he had a keener sense of what wasn't in our purse, and he still had over a year before he would qualify to get a full-time job in his field. As far as I was concerned, all we had to do was seek the kingdom of God first, and all we needed would be added unto us.

When Dan finished his junior year, he was offered a job working for the head of the accounting school for the summer. I had the romantic idea of being a stay-at-home mommy, so I had the chutzpah to tell Dan that I was going to stop working at the coffee shop. My honey seemed a bit hesitant, but he agreed. Somehow we would make it work.

I was happier than I had ever been. Dan went to work early in the morning. I would sit on the old beat-up couch on our front porch, drink herb tea, and read my Bible. For lunch, I packed a picnic basket and walked two blocks to the school. Dan and I sat by the creek, ate our sandwiches, and talked until it was time for him to get back to work.

My afternoons were spent making gifts and refurbishing a large bag of old baby clothes someone had cleared from their attic. They looked like the ones that were around our house when I was a little girl. I washed, mended, and dreamed of the day my baby would wear them. Making a nest for our little olive shoot brought me immeasurable pleasure.

Sometimes Dan and I would walk to the grocery store, towing our wagon. After dinner, we took our evening walk. If we could scrape up enough money, we liked to go to Denny's and share a piece of carrot cake. It was all very romantic.

In September 1979, we brought our baby, Matthew, home to the place we called our hovel. It was run down by many years of being a college residence, with very little maintenance. The front door opened with a squeak and closed with a bang. The uneven wood floors were well worn and painted gray. We hung Indian bedspreads to cover the cracks in the plaster ceilings. There was a hole from dry rot in the floorboards underneath the clawfoot bathtub, and the toilet tank was missing its cover. It was a humble, warm home for our little family.

Even though we had very little money, we felt rich. We had our precious baby boy, a great bunch of friends, and plenty to keep us busy. We were seeking God, and as promised, He was providing all our needs.

My vision was to live in the country. I had dreams of growing vegetables and raising chickens. When I closed my eyes, I saw a place where we could have colorful flowers and clean laundry whipping in the wind. I could almost hear the birds singing in the fields and take in the scent of crisp air. Dan's expressed vision was to get a job as an accountant.

We dreamed of having babies. Conversations of raising a Christian family came up often.

We dreamed of having babies. Conversations of raising a Christian family came up often.

Dan applied to several CPA firms. The best offer was a hundred miles away; therefore, we had to move to "the big city." It didn't fit my picture, but no matter, we looked at it as a grand adventure anyway.

Tearing away from our church family wasn't easy. We had many close relationships. Not being able to see them often was sad for us. They threw us a "fare thee well" party and sent us off with their blessing.

We spent several days melting in the car, baby in tow, searching for something suitable for our budget, a toddler, and our cranky cat. Then hallelujah.

The location was perfect. Dan only had to cross the railroad tracks and the freeway to get to his office. It was a charming 1940s style two-bedroom house, with plenty of space to set up my sewing machine. I was enamored. The dry crabgrass lawn, chipped white paint, and tool shed buried under weeds in the backyard didn't matter.

"Honey, there's already a clothesline for the diapers. The cabinets in the dining room are adorable, and look at the gingerbread molding in the kitchen. It's beautiful, and I love it!"

Our friends and Dan's college professor helped us move in the sweltering heat when the air conditioner was just a promise to be fixed. *God bless these beautiful people for all their hard work.*

Dan worked in his cool office. I spent my days in the living room with Matthew, where I had big fans set up to keep us comfortable. There, I had plenty of time to transform fabric, beads, and trim into tree ornaments. When Dan came home, we headed to the mall to walk along the air-conditioned hallway before heading back to some cold ice cream.

For some reason, my father was unhappy with our neighborhood. He said he wanted us to get away from there. He offered us a down payment so we could buy our own home.

We found a place where my dreams could come true. It was on the edge of the city where the houses had big yards, and livestock of various kinds grazed. The house sat on a quarter acre. There were three bedrooms, two bathrooms, and a fireplace—a home in the country. God heard my heart.

We visited some churches, but it took a while before the shoe seemed to fit. During that time, I read my Bible to Matthew after breakfast and danced around the house with him in my arms while listening to *Keith Green, Second Chapter of Acts, and Randy Stonehill* on the stereo. Matthew would laugh and smile as I twirled him around the room. I listened to Bible studies on Christian radio. The highlight of the day was when Daddy came home. I was in love.

We found our niche in a church a few miles from our home with many people our age and their young families. They sang familiar songs, clapped their hands, and swayed their bodies, just like where we came from. I joined the ladies' Bible study. There were mostly newlyweds and young mothers like me. It was where I met Candy, the leader.

The associate pastor recruited Dan and me to teach first-grade Sunday school. I volunteered to coordinate the scenery and stage props for the Easter Cantata, which proved overwhelming. Fortunately, a guy who knew cabinetry stepped in to help. He built the structure I covered with papier- mâché to make hills for the background.

Since money was tight, I decided to take in some children to babysit during the day. They were a cute preschool brother and sister. All would have been fine, but they brought a nasty flu to our family. We all got so sick we could barely get out of bed for a week. It took a month after that to fully recover.

During that winter, we found out we had another baby on the way. Dan and I were delighted. However, not long after, morning sickness took hold. That made the preparations for the Cantata arduous. I remember the chicken wire and smell of soggy newspaper strips in my cold garage, with my stomach upside down and drained of all energy.

That winter was difficult. I couldn't keep up with the babysitting. After a few months, I told their mother to find someone else. Dan expressed that he wasn't pleased. He didn't want me to be a quit-easy kind of person.

Along with the ladies' Bible study I was part of, Dan and I joined the evening couples' study group. That was where we met Candy's husband, Max. Our group grew to be very close, and we had a lot of good times doing things together.

Spring brought sweet relief. After the Cantata, the flu passed, and the morning sickness subsided. Life was a delight.

In November 1981, we welcomed our new son. We named him Mark. The people in our evening Bible study pulled their dimes together and bought me a cane rocker. It was the source of years of tender moments.

After months of intense study, Dan sat for the CPA exam. He passed all four parts, which was happy news. He still had to put in more work hours and get signed off by his supervisors so he could get his license to practice as a certified public accountant.

A dispute between our friends and the pastor of our church started brewing. It was over how to use the church's money. The pastor was trying to get people to give more because he wanted to fund a more substantial church complex. Our group didn't take kindly to the idea. They had other ideas on how to use the tithes and offerings. *Wouldn't it be better if we used our funds to help those who don't have enough? Or contribute to building up the Sunday school?*

Our group ended up leaving. We stayed close friends but didn't all go to the same church. After trying out a couple of churches, Dan and I grew discouraged and stopped trying.

CHAPTER 2

Blessed Spirit Christian Church

Candy and Max told us about the pastor who had married them. Brad and his wife, Susan, lived in Idaho, where he pastored a church. They had a vision to move back to Sacramento to plant a charismatic church. Max and Candy invited us to his gathering with some of his old friends.

We tagged along so we could hear Brad's ideas. Prayer came first, and then we sang songs. A few I knew already, and there were some beauties I hadn't heard before.

While we sang, the sound of Brad's strumming took me home to Barney and his guitar. The vibe reminded me of our first church.

Brad spoke softly, yet he was strong and direct. His eyes sparkled. He wanted to expand on a traditional liturgy and be open to the movement of the Holy Spirit. They would start as a home church and grow from there. He would break out on his own until he could persuade the Lutheran leadership to embrace his vision. Their coverage was wanted, so his church would not be a lone nomad group and could receive some financial assistance. A tiny grassroots church wouldn't be able to support his family.

Brad's wife, Susan, with her peaches and cream complexion, had a fresh wholesomeness about her. She reminded me of an old-fashioned farmer's wife with a tender, melodious voice. The other women in the house appeared to know her well and talked about how they could form a ladies' Bible study. We decided to meet again after we had time for prayer and to hear from the Holy Spirit. Brad and Susan went back to Idaho so they could get ready to move back to Sacramento.

Dan and I talked while driving home. We discussed the way we felt at home with it. Brad seemed passionate about the Lord. He had contagious exuberance with a warmhearted glimmer in his eye. His vision sounded much closer to what Jesus preached than what we had heard at the last church. That pastor publicly praised someone who donated their wedding ring while he was soliciting funds to pay to build a bigger church.

I looked up to Candy. I had gained respect for her when she was leading the women's Bible study. Max was a nice guy, who was a lot of fun.

"So what do you think?" I asked.

"It sounds grassroots."

"Seems like a bit of an adventure, and Max and Candy wouldn't hook us up with some kook."

"Could be interesting. I'm OK with it if you are."

"Sure, let's do it."

Brad and Susan returned, and we got together again. There were seven couples who were interested in planting Brad's vision. We held our first meeting at one couple's dome-shaped house. Two of the men became our elders. Blessed Spirit Christian Church was born.

In September 1982, we had our first ladies' Bible study. It was the same day I found out I was expecting our third baby. I met Naomi. It happened her little girl had the same birthday as Matthew. She and her family had just moved to the area from a quaint town on the coast. I felt like I could relate to her. We were both young mommies, and we also wore similar clothes, Birkenstocks, and long skirts.

Our mustard seed church began to grow. Candy's two sisters started coming to the dome with their husbands. As word of mouth spread, other couples trickled in. Most of the new people were our age, with budding families.

After a few months, we outgrew the dome. We rented the auditorium and classrooms at the YMCA. We loosely followed a liturgy, prayed together, and sang while Brad played his guitar. We sang some songs new to me and classic old hymns.

Brad and Susan were homegrown country people. We had get-togethers at the ranch of Brad's parents for barbecues amid goats, geese, and farm kitties. We got Mark's milk from their mama goat because he was allergic to everything else.

As my belly grew, Susan took me under her wing. She taught me how to make bread so I could make it for my family. Susan and I grew to be close friends. She was like an elder sister to me.

My heart's desires had come true. I had my honey of a husband, precious young children, and a new one on the way. We had our little brown house with a big yard for our young ones to play in and a vegetable garden. Dan's dad put up a sturdy clothesline for me to hang the diapers out in the sun. Dan had a steady job he loved, which gave us enough income for me to stay home with the children. Our life was complete with lots of church friends and a pastor who had a passion for the Lord.

The time came for me to have my baby. We invited my mother, Brad, Susan, and Naomi to be by my side. Brad quietly played his guitar. After a smooth delivery, it thrilled me to show off our beautiful tiny stocking-capped little girl to the delight of Grandma and our friends.

With the arrival of our little Sarah, we had two boys and a girl. It seemed there was an expectation among our families that now our young family was complete. Our Christian friends' suggestion of letting God determine the size of our family strongly influenced us. Dan and I desired to give our all to God and trust Him to guide our life. Giving up control over the fruit of my womb was our way of saying, "We love You, Lord. Take our family, and do what You will with it." We didn't consider this an act of stupidity but an act of faith. We believed that God would not give us anything more than we could handle.

CHAPTER 3

Wind From Another Direction

Blessed Spirit Christian Church shared the same facilities with another congregation. Their people got out of their cars just as we left the building. It was in passing that Brad met Miguel, the pastor of Tamarisk Covenant Fellowship. They got acquainted and started spending time together.

It wasn't long before there seemed to be a disturbance happening between Brad and the elders of our congregation. They kept the details between themselves, so Dan and I were not aware of what the problem was. I didn't ask questions because I figured it was none of my business. The elders eventually quit coming to our church.

The sunny, easygoing atmosphere of our gatherings faded. There was a subtle tension. Brad's Sunday messages transformed from uplifting and encouraging into more about the fear of God. He preached about the importance of living according to His will to be under His covering.

Like a baby with a bottle before bedtime, I drank what I was fed, taking every word to heart. A vague humidity of fear permeated me.

Miguel's name became commonplace. Our friends spoke about going into counseling with him. They had positive things to say about him helping their marriages. *How wonderful for them, but Dan and I are in no need of a counselor. I'm not interested.*

Brad, Max, and Jackson started wearing baseball caps like Miguel's that had PPK embroidered across the front. It represented a man who was the "prophet, priest, and king" of his home. Brad started repeating the phrase, "No more bozos," which meant a man who wasn't standing up as the spiritual head of his household. It was an insult to be called one. It seemed to perk up men's attention to develop into an active authority in his home.

The wives in counseling with Miguel expressed enthusiasm about how he taught their husbands the importance of loving them and tending to the spiritual needs of their children. They seemed brighter with more zeal for the Lord than they had before.

Before Miguel's influence on Brad, Susan had a dark cloud countenance because she was mourning several miscarriages. Though they were struggling financially, Brad told her to go out and buy some new clothes. Things seemed to look up for her. She seemed encouraged.

One day Dan told me that Brad said I looked "frumpy," so he should buy me some new clothes. Shocked and hurt, I couldn't fathom how our pastor would say something like that to anyone in his congregation. What an awful thing to say about me. I was always conscientious about making sure I dressed clean and neat. We did not have much money for up-to -date fashions. However, I took advantage of the opportunity to freshen up my wardrobe.

Brad placed a significant focus on the scripture, "Wives submit to your own husbands, as to the Lord. For the husband is head of the wife, as also Christ is head of the church; and He is Savior of the body. Therefore, just as the church is subject to Christ, so let the wives be to their own husbands in everything" (Ephesians 5:22–24 [NKJV]). We were told we had to obey our husbands in all things.

The weekly men's breakfast and the Wednesday night Bible study changed from "You're welcome to join us" to "You're expected to be there." The word "mandatory" took root in our everyday vocabulary.

Through it all, more families were joining Blessed Spirit. We grew close, praying, singing, and studying the Word in Brad and Susan's warm, inviting home. Our children were close in age and seemed to enjoy one another's company. Though our church was small, we became like a large family.

⚬❧⚬

Brad called for a retreat at a lodge in Bodega Bay, where Miguel and Sandi liked to stay. He said it was a necessary time for those who were part of Blessed Spirit and serious about giving our lives to God. I had the impression that if we didn't attend, the sincerity of our desire was in question.

A nerve inside me went tense. Something about it being necessary for us to go disturbed me, yet my desire to show the Lord that I meant business about following Him pushed those feelings aside.

A question about if a Christian was sincerely dedicated floated between the lines of much of what Brad and our friends talked about. We had discussions about what was called greasy grace. It meant going to church but not completely submitted to the Lord.

While we were in Bodega Bay, Brad drew an umbrella to demonstrate God's will for His people. Brad said we need to be under His covering to receive His promises and protection. Then he explained how God uses His delegates to guide and direct His flock. He talked about how Christians need to be obedient to truly follow Him. If we are not "under authority," we cannot be in God's will.

I had a tight feeling in my gut, but the things he said seemed to make sense. I overruled my emotion, thinking that the Lord was just testing my faithfulness.

Brad gave us a copy of a Christian book about God's authority. The author had knowledge of the Bible far beyond mine. He seemed to have a very dynamic walk with the Lord and sought to follow Jesus with all his heart.

The book said that God delegates His authority through governmental agencies, church leaders, bosses, husbands, fathers, mothers, etc. He executes His will using those over us and expects heartfelt obedience from His disciples. Throughout the book, the author uses scripture to back the points he's trying to make.

Brad gave us this book to read to reinforce that we needed someone to be over us, and we should be subservient to our church leaders. Giving up our wills to follow our pastor was how we were to die to ourselves and live for Christ Jesus.

When we received a direction, we had to do what we were told without argument. Questioning was rebellion, which is "as the sin of witchcraft" (1 Samuel 15:23 [NKJV]). If the person in authority was making a mistake, it was supposedly their responsibility. They had to face the consequences. It was our place to be compliant.

The book said we shouldn't uncover our leader's flaws. Ham did when Noah got drunk. In Genesis 9:21–25, it says that Ham saw his drunken father as he lay naked in his tent. He told his brothers Shem and Japheth. They took a garment and walked backward with it so they could cover their father without looking upon his nakedness. When Noah woke up and saw what Ham had done, he spoke a curse on him.

Jesus said, "Assuredly I say to you, unless you are converted and become as little children, you will by no means enter the kingdom of heaven" (Matthew 18:3 [NKJV]). We were like that, trusting our elders in the Lord and following the Bible as it was presented to us. I loved the Lord as well as feared Him. I wanted to please Him, not anger or disappoint Him. Since Brad was our pastor, I thought we were being called by God to obey him. That is how we showed that we wanted to be God's children and could receive His covering.

CHAPTER 4

Meanwhile

We were instructed to read our Bibles, worship, and pray on our own every day. When we got together at Brad and Susan's house during the week, we concentrated on Jesus's death on the cross to take the punishment for our sins. There was also a lot of encouragement to produce the fruit of the Holy Spirit, be loving and forgiving toward others, and many other things common in Christian churches.

Brad and the others who were seeing Miguel for counseling seemed to be ahead of Dan and me. I saw them as being more mature in the Lord. They were getting more acquainted with the people in Tamarisk Covenant Fellowship. From what we were hearing from them, the fellowship had a passion for the Lord.

I was preoccupied with starting to homeschool Matthew. Dan and I wanted our children to have a Christian-based education. We had no extra money for a private school. Also, I was concentrating on studying the theory that it was better to start a child's formal studies later than the norm. I identified with the "better late than early" movement. I wanted to have a home-based school that integrated learning how to read, write, and work on math concepts, science, and social studies with regular home and church-based activities. I had the vision to develop a cottage industry to blend with what I was teaching my children.

The Tamarisk members were pooling their resources to run a cooperative school. I didn't know much about it. Though it sounded interesting, my heart was on building my homeschool.

I wasn't enthusiastic about intermingling with the Tamarisk people. Deep down, I was dragging my feet. It appeared the Lord was leading us in that direction, but something inside me made me want to maintain my distance. However, I questioned whether my feeling might be because I had a rebellious attitude toward "coming under authority." According to what we were taught, the answer to the question was yes.

Tamarisk Covenant Fellowship invited our church to join them for a worship service. *I don't feel like it, but it sounds reasonable. Why not?*

The atmosphere in the auditorium was highly charged compared with our services. Everyone seemed focused and determined. They were friendly with us while at the same time, there was a vague tension in the air. The singing was enthusiastic like I had never witnessed before. There were songs I was familiar with, some not. Miguel preached with authority. He reminded me of a commander speaking to his troops.

All the women wore a scarf on their heads, including us. Brad brought up the scripture that talks about women wearing them during prayer. We had to wear them at church and Bible studies.

I recalled that back in the Chico days, I approached our pastor Barney with what the Bible says about a woman having her head covered. "But every woman who prays or prophesies with her head uncovered dishonors her head, for that is just the same as if her head were shaved. For if a woman is not covered, let her be shorn. But if it is shameful for a woman to be shorn or shaved, let her be covered" (1Corinthians 11:5–6 [NKJV]).

I cannot remember what his response was. It still seemed like a head-scratcher to me. I didn't see any Christian churches doing it except some old-school Catholics. From this, I deduced that the Tamarisk people took what was written in the Bible very seriously.

I was all for it. It reminded me of the Amish people, which is something that had always attracted me. I saw them as people who were extra dedicated to the Lord, like the nuns who taught me before I went through catechism. I thought of becoming one for a while, but my desire to get married and have a family was much stronger. I told God that I wanted to be like a nun except have a husband and children. I felt God was good with the idea.

When our little girl, Sarah, was around seven months old, Susan was in her fifth month of pregnancy. Her heart's desire was to have another child. She noticed she felt no movement after the baby had been very active. Terrified of losing another one, she called her doctor.

Susan's worst fear met reality. The doctor could not find a heartbeat. A sonogram confirmed that her child had died. She was advised to go home and wait to see if she would begin to deliver on her own. A few days of devastation later, her doctor said she would have to have her labor induced.

My heart broke for her. The thought of her having to go through labor to deliver her dead baby was horrible. I asked her if she would like me to be there to support her through it. She said she would be grateful.

Brad, Susan, and I went to the hospital together. The nurse began inducing her labor. When the time to deliver was eminent, a nurse came into the room with a large white bucket. I was appalled! *What a heart-stabbing thing to do.*

Susan sadly asked if I could have the nurse bring a receiving blanket. I found a different nurse and explained the situation to her. A few minutes after she brought it, Susan was holding her stillborn son in it.

Brad spoke softly. "His name is John."

The time we spent sitting there with the baby was palpable bittersweet. When Susan and Brad said they were ready, the nurse tenderly picked him up and carried him away.

The closest contact I had with Miguel was the day I heard him from behind the pulpit. The man whom I heard so many awesome things about walked into Susan's hospital room. He had a significant presence—very businesslike. He asked if she would like something to eat. After making a phone call to tell someone from his church to bring her what she requested, he told Brad to go with him to get some coffee.

Who does he think he is? He sure takes charge, ordering people around.

After that day, I felt uptightness building inside me. Sarah developed an adverse reaction to my milk. I kept nursing her for a while. She continued to have distressing digestive symptoms. It was hard for me because I had to give her goat's milk instead.

Somewhere within this time frame, Brad approached Dan and told him that we should see Miguel for counseling. I bristled like a threatened cat.

"What? Why does Brad think we need counseling? We don't need it."

"I don't know. He just said we should."

"So what? Tell him we aren't interested."

"I think it might be a good thing, and he wants us to."

"We don't need it. Tell him no."

"I'm not going to tell him no."

I continued to object, but it was no use. Dan wouldn't budge.

I was furious. The thought of sitting in a room, the focus of Miguel's attention, frightened and sickened me. Rebelling against God was worse. It was better to be on the safe side and comply.

The dreaded evening arrived. Brad, Dan, and me climbed the stairs to Miguel's office. It was as if I was about to have my soul stripped, examined, and judged.

The four of us talked while Miguel leaned back in his office chair with his hands folded behind his head. Our conversation is a blur to me except he told me that my problem wasn't rebellion; it was fear. When the meeting was over, he said I needed to go for deliverance from my demons.

A few weeks after our chat with Miguel, Brad told Dan that we needed to continue to see Miguel for counseling. I argued with Dan, repeating the same arguments I had the first time. Dan said he wanted me to go to help me with problems that haunted me from my childhood. He said he was at a loss as to how to help. Though I knew what he was talking about, I still had no interest in seeking Miguel for help.

When Dan wouldn't budge from his position, I broke into a panicked rage. I screamed and cried so hard I burst blood vessels in my eyes. Dan went quiet.

The next day, Dan told me Miguel said that if I felt so strongly against it, I didn't have to go. I was deeply grateful that God heard my cry.

CHAPTER 5

Deliverance?

Though I didn't have to continue counseling with Miguel, I still had to go for deliverance. This force -fed my anxiety. One thing that held me back was the big deal they made about confessing sins. I had some relationships before we got married Dan didn't know about. They were something I was very ashamed of and had told myself I would never tell him.

"Confess your trespasses to one another, and pray for one another, that you may be healed. The effective, fervent prayer of a righteous man avails much" (James 5:16 [NKJV]).

One night I unveiled my past. Dan also opened the door to things he had hidden from me. It was an intimate and bittersweet time of releasing our shame and receiving acceptance and forgiveness. Through it, the bond between us grew stronger.

I still had to face going through deliverance. Brad gave me a book about why and how to set people free from demons. Reading it did little to relieve my mind about baring my soul to an elder from Tamarisk Covenant Fellowship. I wanted to run away.

Foreboding twisted my stomach sideways as Brad drove Dan and me to the house where the event was to take place. They led me into a room built into the elder's, Larry's, garage. His wife, Roxy, a lady whom I had enjoyed getting to know at a previous women's breakfast, came to be a female witness. Her warm eyes and sweet smile gave me some comfort.

We started with prayer. Larry called upon Jesus to cover all of us with His blood and claimed power over the demons. He used a list he had of the different types. One by one, he named them and called them to come out of me. That was when things got strange.

My body began to jerk and twist. My eyes widened and darted around. I didn't know what was happening to me. Larry told me to cough the demons out as he commanded them to leave. Brad, Roxy, and Dan sat watching. This went on for a few hours. When Larry had gone down his list, he led us in prayer to thank Jesus for cleansing me and asked the Lord to fill me with His Holy Spirit. Besides my strange reactions, it was all done in a calm way.

When we left, it was a tremendous relief that it was over. Dan said it freaked him out to watch me writhe around as I did. The next couple of days, I was woozy and confused. *Was it demons that caused me to behave like that, or was I hypnotized?*

CHAPTER 6

The Rod of Correction

One night during our midweek flock meeting, Brad passed out a pamphlet. It was their introduction to how to "train up a child in the way he should go …" (Proverbs 22:6 [NKJV]). Discipline became a focus during our Bible studies for a while. He brought up several verses in the Bible that referred to using a rod to correct children. "He who spares his rod hates his son, but he who loves him disciplines him diligently" (Proverbs 13:24 [NKJV]). "Foolishness is bound up in the heart of a child; the rod of correction will drive it far from him" (Proverbs 22:15 [NKJV]). "Do not withhold correction from a child, for if you beat him with a rod, he will not die. You shall beat him with a rod and deliver his soul from hell" (Proverbs 23:13–14 [NKJV]). We were told to use a wooden paddle for a rod.

Dan and I believed we were learning how God wanted us to discipline our children. Brad coached us to make sure our kids understood what they did that was wrong and why and then swat them on their backside one time. After that, and they apologized, we were to reinforce love and forgiveness toward them.

I have early childhood memories of violence between my parents. When I was three years old, my mother left my father. After that, they shuffled my siblings and me back and forth between two very different households. Life had a bad-dream quality to it. I felt much safer with my mother, but there was never any real peace because my parents continued to fight. My father never left her alone.

I dreaded being with my father. I escaped his terrible temper by making myself quiet and cooperative. When he didn't like my behavior, like poor table manners or minor mistakes, he would blame my brothers for not keeping an eye on me to make sure I knew better. They would get reprimanded instead of me. When my father remarried, there was the constant threat of loud fights that could escalate to striking blows. I remember one time my stepmother pulled out a chef's knife to defend herself. Life with my mother was different. She was easygoing and loving. However, she had a lot on her shoulders and was frequently preoccupied or exhausted. She worked hard but slept excessively. Though she wasn't always an all-present parent, I knew she loved me. She comforted and protected me.

Our family was Catholic. My parents didn't go to church but made sure I received my first communion and, later, my confirmation. I attended church services yet didn't grasp the meaning of the gospel or have any understanding of what it meant to live a Christian life.

With how to raise godly children, I was all ears. The coaching we received from Brad seemed loving and predictable compared with what I had grown up with. It sounded all right to me because it wasn't arbitrary or motivated by anger. The method was consistent. Dan and I bought into the program.

When we were getting used to using the rod, how hard to swat came up. Brad criticized some couples for being too soft-handed. He said it was better to ere by being too tough on a child than too easy.

We were told not to be afraid of leaving bruises. That seemed harsh to me. I assumed I was wrong and took what Brad said as God's way.

The subject of Child Protective Services came up. We were told they were "of the world," therefore against God's way of handling children. The members of the fellowship feared them because of the threat of them finding out we were using a rod on our kids. We believed they would take our kids away from us.

CHAPTER 7

Commitment

Tamarisk Covenant Fellowship considered themselves to be a covenant community. Members had to agree that as a pastor, God anointed Miguel to keep watch over the church. Miguel's pastor lived in the Los Angeles area.

To become a part of the group, you had to stand in front of the congregation and take a solemn oath accepting the covering of a delegated authority to lead and guide you. By taking the vow, you agreed to stay with the group until separated by death. The covenant relationship was like marrying a church.

Brad made a formal covenant with Miguel. Blessed Spirit became one of Tamarisk's "flocks." Brad was "in authority" over his congregation.

Up to this point, Dan hadn't made any formal agreement with Brad. However, we still functioned as if he did. The only difference was we couldn't attend any of the "covenant meetings," which they held separately from the regular worship services.

Brad became increasingly dominant over us. His suggestions turned into orders.

When I was seven months along with our fourth child, my stepfather suddenly passed away. I was homeschooling Matthew, so I could bring the children to Tahoe to be with my mom. We wanted to be together while she dealt with the shock and handled all the final arrangements.

It was tax season. Dan had to work late into the night, so he said I could stay with my mom for as long as she needed me. It helped him because he didn't have all of us waiting for him at home.

I set up our homeschool at my mother's. The children and I settled in to stay with her until she returned to work and felt like she could handle things alone.

One day I received a phone call from Brad. He informed me that the Blessed Spirit flock was having a barbecue on his parents' ranch the next day.

"I'm sorry, I can't make it. I can't leave my mother just yet."

"I don't think you understand. You must come and be part of it."

"No, Brad, my mom still needs me to help her get through this."

"Florentine, I'm saying that you don't have a choice in the matter."

I couldn't believe what he was telling me. My face got hot, and my heart started pounding.

"You've got to be kidding me! You're ordering me to come home? Now? When my mother just lost her husband?" I yelled.

"Yes. You have to come home."

By this time, I was livid.

"Dan says it's good for me to be up here."

"No, you have to come. Dan needs you."

"No, he doesn't. He's focused on work."

"Trust me. He needs you to be near him. 'Let the dead bury their own dead.'" (Matthew 8:22 [NKJV])

When I hung up, I was in tears. I had a choice—obey my shepherd or do what everything inside me wanted. It's the Lord testing me to see how much I love Him. Am I willing to lay down my life and die to myself? The thought of leaving my mother turned my stomach, and the prospect of disobeying God scared my bone marrow.

Mom seemed disappointed but understanding when I said Dan needed me at home. She told me not to feel bad because I had been with her for two weeks. Her words of gratitude and warm smile helped little to ease my twisted heart.

I was already home when Dan came in from work. He stopped in his tracks.

"What are you doing here?"

His jaw fell when I told him Brad said I should be home with him because he needed me. He seemed puzzled and said I should have stayed with my mother.

Still, it was good to be home with my honey. I accepted the circumstances as the way it had to be, but I was counting the cost. It was a rude awakening as to how much control I had lost over my life.

CHAPTER 8

Getting in Deeper

As we became more familiar with the Tamarisk way of life, our eyes opened to their fasting. It was mandatory, which appalled me. I dreaded it.

Our introduction occurred when Dan and I were having our house hooked up to the city sewer. Our backyard had a mountain of dirt that had to go back in the trench. Brad organized a work party for men to come over and help us get the job done.

However, the weekend Brad scheduled them to come over was toward the end of the Tamarisk annual seven-day, water-only fast. Those white -faced, sweating servants finished the job. At least he was out there shoveling in the heat with them.

Blessed Spirit started joining all of Tamarisk's worship services and activities. They still looked upon us as outsiders, so along with not being allowed to attend their covenant meetings, our family could not take part in their cooperative school. I was okay with that since I had no desire at that point to be part of the school.

One night after a worship service, when everyone headed out to their cars, one of the Tamarisk women called my name. I didn't know who she was. When she caught up to me, she handed me a piece of paper. It looked like a schedule, which puzzled me.

"What's this?"

"It's the coop cleaning schedule."

"What? There's been a mistake. Why are you giving it to me? My kids aren't part of the school."

"I don't have any children, and I have to do it."

Without further argument, I took the list and showed it to Dan. He looked it over and said he would call Brad. I was in his ear about it all the way home. "Who do they think they are, signing me up for something without consulting me about it? We're not even part of the covenant!"

When the babes were in bed for the night, Dan phoned Brad. They talked for several minutes.

"Well, what did he say?"

"You have to clean the co- op, along with the other ladies."

"That's crazy!" I yelled. "Tell Brad no."

"I won't do that. I'm sorry, you've got to do it anyway."

Tears wet my hot cheeks. I continued to argue my point, but it was no use.

He wouldn't budge.

Unbeknownst to my honey, they put him on the men's work schedule. He was part of the rotating team of men who had to mow the lawns of Miguel and two of his elders. He also got to do his share to clean and wax the school's floors.

That was the end. It seemed I had to pry my shaky fingers off governing my time and energy. It no longer belonged to me. I had to give it whenever they asked. Or?

Like others who had balked at following orders, we could end up confronted for our attitude toward serving the Lord. If we didn't repent, we would be shamed and cast out from under their covering, for the destruction of our flesh. The other children would not be allowed to interact with ours.

Dreadful as that would be for our family, it was worse to think of being out from under God's protection. We believed we would be open to the devil's attack until we repented. Only then would they allow us back into the fold.

CHAPTER 9

Save the Babies

Brad and Susan were big on families and having as many children as God saw fit to send. However, they didn't lord this over us. They saw the issue as one for a couple to determine. Dan and I relinquished my womb to God.

With Brad submitted to Miguel's influence, he had a contagious passion for the pro-life movement. Brad showed us horrible pictures of aborted babies. He passed around articles about the different aspects of the pro-life movement.

Blessed Spirit joined Tamarisk's militant stand against abortion. We passed out flyers for pro-life candidates running for public office. Every Saturday we rotated to give pamphlets to women entering an abortion clinic. Our goal was to encourage them to think it over again and offer them help.

One pro-choice organization held an annual antique sale to raise money. It became another one of our yearly activities. We showed up to picket against them. While we were on the sidewalk, we had a truck circling the area carrying an enormous picture of a mangled, aborted baby.

One year Miguel got even more dramatic. He had us do our usual picketing. Another group from our church showed up dressed in black, with creepy, zombie-looking, black-and-white face paint. Each one wore a red armband. One of them pushed a wheelbarrow containing torn apart dolls covered in fake blood. There was a tape of a baby crying hidden under them. Years later, one of those picketers told me Miguel picked her to be in this group. She said that Miguel had a phlebotomist from the church, draw blood from them. They used the blood to paint the signs they carried.

We had to take part in these activities, rain or shine. I recall a year when it was pouring rain. It was cold and miserable. When we got home, we were shivering and soaked down through our underwear.

There was a twenty- four-hour pregnancy crisis line. We set up a forwarding system and took turns handling the calls. It was our goal to talk the women into saving their babies. We were there to help in whatever way we could, including giving the mother a place to live. There were a handful of women who took the church up on their offer. Dan and I housed no one, but we deterred one young lady from choosing to take her baby's life.

Boycotting was big. We were told not to buy anything from any company that supported proabortion organizations. The list was extensive and required us to go out of our way to avoid shopping at certain stores. It was a bummer, but Dan and I believed in the cause, so we didn't resent having to comply.

There was a movement to stop seeing any doctors who performed or referred for abortion. The families in the fellowship were told to check with their doctors. If they either performed or referred their patients for an abortion, we were mandated to leave them.

We loved our doctor. He was our physician since I was pregnant with our second child. He delivered Mark. Our children had never been to another doctor. It was like he was part of our family.

Conflicted, I approached Dan about it.

"Honey, should we ask Dr. Yee about the abortion issue?"

"I'm not concerned about it. He's only a primary care physician and doesn't perform them."

"Yes, but what if he will send a patient to someone who will?"

"Dr. Yee is a good man. I don't think we should bother confronting him."

"But I'll feel guilty if we don't."

"You can ask him if you want to."

"I don't want to. What if he does? We'll have to leave him."

"If you don't want to, just let it drop. There's no reason to feel you have to just because everybody else is."

Because Dan had authority over me, I reasoned that I was obedient to him as my spiritual head. However, I carried subliminal guilt that kept popping its head up. I feared God would punish Dan for not being compliant. I kept having to put it out of my mind.

CHAPTER 10

Some Sugar

Once I resigned myself to our pastor's authority, I spent much of my attention on enjoying the relationships that were growing in our church family. We had a lot in common. One of those things was the high regard we placed on bearing children. The more, the better.

Susan was pregnant again. We were all excited for her because her pregnancy had gone smoothly, and she was approaching her due date. Annabelle and I were also in our third trimester. I was getting ready to have my fourth. Since our babies were due near the same time, we delighted in our little ones kicking and squirming and timing our Braxton-Hicks contractions while wondering who would deliver first.

First, we celebrated with Susan and Brad. They were jubilant over their darling baby girl. She was a radiant light that chased away the darkness of mourning their stillborn son.

Our quiver expanded with our fourth son, Luke. We had three boys and a girl for a seventh anniversary present the day he was born. My honey and I felt thoroughly blessed.

Just hours after he was born, Jackson and Anabelle arrived at the hospital. When I was up and walking around, I snuck off the postpartum floor and discretely stood outside her room while she delivered her new son. It was fun to chat with our friends, holding our bundles in Annabelle's hospital room. I will always remember the joyous occasion.

When a Tamarisk woman was having a baby, there was always someone to care for her children. Then for two weeks, they provided homemade dinners for her family. Even though we hadn't become covenanted members, they blessed our family with meals. My mother enjoyed talking with the people in the fellowship when they came to bring us our dinners.

Through times such as this, a precious bond developed with the people in our flock and the Tamarisk community.

After our family adjusted to include Luke in our daily activities, I continued to work on building the framework for our homeschool. Matthew was entering his kindergarten year. I wanted to be sure he kept up with the things other children were learning, so I ordered a Christian-based curriculum. I set up lesson plans and attendance records. With all kinds of learning materials and teacher's aides at our fingertips, we dug in.

Though Matthew's learning activities were the general focus, I also involved our other children in what we did. We read a lot of stories and books related to social studies and science. While Matthew and Mark still weren't able to write, I took dictation as they told their stories and relayed to me what they wanted to say in letters to relatives. The math manipulatives were a source of fun for all. We gardened, cooked, and did all kinds of art projects while Luke would crawl around and do his baby things.

The other mothers in the fellowship were busy working together to set up their co-op Christian school. I stayed on the periphery, listening when they talked. It all sounded interesting, but I was glad not to have to be so deeply ingrained with the Tamarisk program.

CHAPTER 11

Speaking Truth

Tamarisk had an annual tradition. When school broke for Christmas vacation, they headed for a retreat in the mountains called Harding Crest. There, the adults fasted water only for three days to seek what the Holy Spirit was saying to the church. Since only those "in the covenant" could take part, our family couldn't attend.

What a relief. To be stuck in close quarters with them was dreadful. The thought of three days without food made me cringe. The last time I fasted was during the throes of being anorexic as a teenager. It's something I had no interest in feeling again.

Upon their return, Dan and I hosted a dinner for the people in the Blessed Spirit flock. Everyone who had gone seemed excited. They had new insight into what the Lord expects from His followers. The big thing was "speaking the truth to one another."

It sounded like we weren't supposed to censor our thoughts and feelings before expressing them. We were to speak our minds without holding back. Supposedly by doing so, the Body of Christ would cleanse itself.

I was mortified. My thoughts could be damaging or humiliating. There was no way I wanted to be so candid. The kinds of things that could cross my mind could be harmful and embarrassing. Where's room for second thoughts? What happened to controlling our tongues?

I looked up to these people. They seemed to have a new awakening that I wasn't grasping. I wanted the days before I ever got involved with this movement. Ignorance was bliss. I wanted to live like other Christians. I wished that what I believed before was the truth.

As I laid in bed that night, my stomach burned. Walking according to what we were being taught was dreadful. Every time I turned, I was told to go a direction I resisted. *But how can I go back?* A voice in my head spoke ominously. *"If you walk away, you're refusing to listen to what God is telling you. He's calling you forward. Your resistance is your flesh, not wanting to die. If you're going to follow in Jesus's footsteps, you must crucify your flesh, and like Jesus, say, 'Not my will, but Thine be done.'"*

My spirit grieved. *But I want to be with Jesus. What if all this is true? Then leaving would mean I'm not worthy of being called a Christian. I would be walking out from under His covering, where there's no protection from Satan. That would mean hell and damnation for all eternity.*

I was a mouse caught in a corner, facing the eyes of a cat.

I didn't have the courage to verify what I heard that night. What if what I thought I heard was true? I was afraid to ask. If the answer was yes, then I would be forced to make a decision I was not ready to face. Better not to know for sure. Then I could still hope I had misinterpreted it. I placed the issue in the back of my mind, telling myself that I would just observe how it played out in the days to come.

CHAPTER 12

The Fateful Decision

Homeschooling went smoothly at first, but as the year progressed, Matthew's work was more demanding and structured. He was uncooperative at times, which made it harder to keep up with my lesson plans. I wasn't equipped as a mom for dealing with a child with strong-willed tendencies. We ended up getting into power struggles, which drew us away from the positive energy we needed for our school to be successful.

Matthew was learning his basics, but I was wondering how things would go in the long run. Because we were so isolated, I questioned if he had enough social interaction. Deep down in my heart, I knew he would fare better if he had someone else as his teacher.

I visited the Tamarisk elementary school. They had converted a garage into a charming classroom filled with educational and fun materials. They set the backyard up with play equipment for the kids to enjoy during recesses. The head teacher had her teaching degree. Mothers took turns helping her with the reading and math groups as well as other subjects. With only six students in the class, there were more teachers than children. I thought it was terrific.

It looked like having Matthew in the school would be an ideal situation. It was a Christian school. Someone else would see to it he was learning the same things as his age-mates, and he would get much needed social interactions under the watchful eyes of dedicated mothers.

I still had my reservations about getting more deeply entrenched with the Tamarisk people, but it seemed like God was leading us in that direction. I thought my flesh was pulling me away from what the Lord wanted me to do. "Most assuredly I say to you unless a grain of wheat falls into the ground and dies, it remains alone; but if it dies, it produces much grain. He who loves his life will lose it, and he who hates his life in this world will keep it for eternal life" (John 12:24–25 [NKJV]).

I wanted to follow Jesus. He didn't want to be beaten and murdered on a cross. In the garden, before He died, Jesus prayed, saying, "Father, if it is Your will, take this cup away from Me; nevertheless, not My will but Yours be done" (Luke 22:42 [NKJV]). No one told me to die on a cross. Who was I to complain? I was only asked to give up running my life as I saw fit.

My doubts about continuing to run our homeschool, the pleasant view I had of the Tamarisk school, and all that seemed to motion us into community life together landed us at a crossroad. If we wanted our children be a part of the school, we had to be in covenant with them.

Our resistance seemed to be putting us at odds with what the Lord wanted. We knew that joining the group would be a commitment to walk with them for the rest of our lives. It was a sober situation to consider.

Dan and I talked it through.

"What do you think, honey? Are you willing to commit to these people for the rest of our lives?"

"You'll be the one most involved with the school. Do you really want to do that?"

"I think it would be what's best for the children. They will grow up surrounded by other Christian families and have a quality education. I will be right there in the classroom with them."

"You're up to it?"

"Until I think about the 'till death do you part' bit. I swallow hard on that."

"Yes. I get that, but it seems to be what the Lord is telling us to do."

Would Dan be saying that if the Lord didn't want it? I want this pull in me to go away. If I say yes, the tug-of-war will be over.

Dan and Brad stood in front of the congregation one Sunday. Miguel was with them. He led them in a prayer for their commitment to one another. He asked the Lord to bless them as they spoke their obligations to one another. I can't remember what they said, but I can still hear the clapping and whistling.

CHAPTER 13

Moving Forward

With the decision made and the sacred oath spoken, we were committed to this body of believers. Leaving the sanctuary that day, a part of me felt at peace. Whether to join was laid to rest.

They reeled us into community life. They held our first of countless covenant meetings after a Sunday worship service. The few who were not members gathered their things and meandered their way out of the sanctuary.

The mothers hurried to the nursery and Sunday schools to check on their children. The sound of the metal chairs banging against one another echoed. The men rearranged them from two rows with an aisle into a big circle. The children remained in their classrooms, and the teenagers took charge of them. After we settled the young ones down with their lunches, everyone went into the multipurpose room that served as our sanctuary. Everyone seemed to know exactly what they were doing except us, so as they found a seat and sat facing one another, we followed suit. The room went quiet.

Wide-eyed, curious, and half cringing, I wondered what would happen. The people started praying out loud in their prayer language.

After that went on for a few minutes, Miguel called the meeting to order.

Structured under Robert's Rules, the conversation was orderly. It was likely to be issues about plans that were being organized. It could have been about the school, work parties, political issues, outreaches such as the pregnancy crisis line, and the tamale feed. Given the time of year, we likely talked about the fellowship's annual talent show. The year before, Brad told me I was "typecast" into the role of the shrew in Shakespeare's *Taming of the Shrew*.

The gathering was about two hours long. As time passed, some meetings could drag on until it was time to go home and fix dinner. They could be depressing and exhausting, depending on what was on the agenda. *Well, that wasn't so bad—just business, but for two hours?* "Ugh."

Now members, we had to take part in the fellowship's annual trip to Bodega Bay, an event that took place at the end of every school year. Families packed up a week's worth of camping gear and took over the upper section of a campground by the ocean. Some people had RVs, while others used tents. The kids brought their trikes, bikes, and toys and used the big circle of camps as their playground while the adults lounged, hanging out and visiting one another. A handful of people would go out and dive for abalone. When they returned, the whole fellowship would work together to prepare an abalone feed for all.

Some families loved the camp trip. Over time, I grew to dread it. I wasn't fond of sleeping on the ground and damp sand with several children. We always had one in diapers and, at times, one under my belt.

I recall the awful day after we would get home. At least ten loads of damp, sandy laundry waited for me to sort and bag up. The children would scurry around being themselves while I packed all the washables into our van. We would all pile in and off to the laundromat we'd go.

I was a mom with her bustling brood, doing what it took to get all that stuff washed, dried, folded, sorted, and loaded back into the van. After we dropped that off at the house, we'd head to the grocery store.

Then came fixing dinner and making sure the kids got their baths. At the tail end of this, we all went to bed.

Our first year at Bodega Bay, Matthew and I were getting ready to start in at Tamarisk Christian School. Miguel's wife, Sandi, a special education teacher for our local school district, serving as the principal, summoned me to her RV. She said she wanted me to be Ms. Sherry's teacher's aide while she taught reading and math. I would have the class to myself for social studies. She told me to see Sherry so she could give me the lesson plans.

We talked about the preschool testing and what that entailed. Sandi said that she wanted Matthew and Mark tested along with the others. The idea of testing Mark hit hard. *What? Mark? He's only four years old!* I was afraid to cross her.

Seething, I told Dan about the situation. He agreed about Mark but wasn't as adamant about it. Upset though I was, I kept my thoughts between Dan and myself.

The kids were checked out thoroughly to gather what they knew and where their strengths and weaknesses were. It turned out that Matthew would join his age-mates in the first grade. Mark tested ready for kindergarten. Sandi said I could have him start school if I wanted or keep him home another year because of his age. I was one happy mommy that day. Mark could stay home, where my heart was shouting he belonged.

CHAPTER 14

School

I met with Sherry to talk about social studies. She told me I would teach the history of transportation. While I was wrapping my mind around what that might entail, she handed me a one-inch thick packet of faded photocopies bound with a single metal ring.

"I used these as a guide. The kids do a special project." She pointed to the papers. "They build little wooden trucks. You'll find the instructions in here." I thumbed through the stack. Most of it was hard to read. I saw the plans for the truck. They looked simple except I knew close to nothing about working with wood, a hammer, and nails. I had trouble imagining what it would be like to lead six six-year-olds through that project.

It took a couple of days before I grasped that the plans Sherry gave me were close to useless. I had to figure out a way to make the history of transportation last the school year and be engaging for Matthew and his schoolmates. It was something different from what I ever experienced before. Since it was still the beginning of summer, I had time to figure out how to put together a curriculum. That was back in the day before the Internet. At the library, I learned about the subject from Adam and

Eve walking in the garden all the way to space travel. I found a lot of books that cultivated ideas. I broke it all down into forty-five-minute lessons that would be informative and entertaining. By the end of the term, I had a complete set of lesson plans for future use.

The married women in the fellowship didn't have jobs outside of the home. They pressed the ones who had jobs into quitting to support the school effort as teachers, babysitters, or both. I was scheduled to work at the school for three days and babysit two.

I became a very busy mom. Planning and preparing for school, plus the time it took me to drop my little ones off at the sitter, besides caring for my family drove me to work harder than ever. I poured myself into doing the best job I could. I didn't want my family or housekeeping to suffer.

A typical school day started around five thirty in the morning. I made sure everyone was fed. Dan and I made sure the children got dressed and ate breakfast. I was bent on keeping our home neat and organized. The beds were made, rooms put in order, and dishes washed. With lunches packed and all necessities in backpacks, we loaded into the car at seven forty-five. It took a half hour to get to the babysitter's house to drop off my three youngest, before Matthew and I headed to school a few miles away.

The class started at eight thirty. We began with prayer requests and singing to the Lord. With the Pledge of Allegiance said, the children sat and started with reading. Based on the preschool assessment, we divided the students into two groups. Ms. Sherry led the class, and I helped the students along. Then the kids went out into the backyard for recess.

After the break, it was time for math. Again, I was an aide. The reason for me to assist Ms. Sherry was twofold. Each child could get individual support, and I observed so I could learn to teach it myself.

When lunch was over, I had the class for social studies. I tried to incorporate other things they were learning along with their lessons.

I read books, and the class took part in group dictation to retell what they learned. We did countless art projects and went on many field trips to coincide with the units we were studying. I took photos of our various activities and made copies for each student. We put the reports and many of the art projects in scrapbooks so all of them could have their own to keep.

I wrote all my lesson plans and included lists of books and needed materials for each project. I didn't want me or anyone else to have to do the prep work all over again. It was important to me to make it much easier in the coming years.

When the school day ended, Matthew and I would pick up the rest of my babies from the babysitter. We got home around three in the afternoon. I'd get the children settled, and then it was time for homework.

Tamarisk School demanded a lot from the students. Homework was a significant part of the day. Even the kindergarten had reading and math assignments every school night. Penmanship had to be meticulous. Though moms helped the kids with the work, the fathers had to oversee to make sure they did everything that was expected. They had to sign each piece and the assignment tag to show their approval. If there were problems, it was Dad's responsibility to communicate them to the teacher who gave the assignment.

Before we got involved with the school, I would frequently read to my kids in the evening. However, with all the concentration on keeping up with schoolwork, extra reading fell by the wayside. There were only so many hours in the day. I struggled to keep up with all that needed to get done. It was a challenge.

CHAPTER 15

Birdseed

We finally reached a financial comfort zone where we could think about buying a van. Up to that time, Brad and Susan were generous enough to loan us theirs when we took trips out of town to see our relatives. I was looking forward to when we would be ready to look for one. I was tired of riding wedged between the front and back seat of our Ford Granada. Dan and the children occupied the seat belts.

We had another major inconvenience. We lived a solid half-hour drive from the babysitter. Add to that the ten-minute drive to get to the school. The commute took a big chunk out of the precious hours of my home time, which added stress to my housekeeping and mothering. I was getting edgy with the kids, trying to keep up with my tightened schedule. My agenda was infringing on my ability to keep things light with room for being able to relax with my young ones.

Dan brought the issues to Brad for discussion. He thought moving closer to the school should be our priority. It would give me more time as well as a bigger house for our growing family. I was happy with our house but very frustrated with riding around like the inside of a sandwich. I leaned more toward getting a van. I thought it was more pressing. Brad had a solution. He said we should get our house ready to sell. He knew of someone in the fellowship who had an old VW up for sale.

At first sight, it looked like it had seen much better days. Its red color looked like it had endured years of baking in the hot summer sun and being washed by the cold winter rains. The interior was in good condition, considering how old it was, but you could see the ground beneath it where the pedals joined with the floor. The cherry on the cake was a tire bolted to the front. It had no cover. It looked like a big, black, ugly nose. This did not appeal to my aesthetic desires. However, it was in decent running condition, and our family could easily fit into it. It was affordable. Our transportation dilemma solved.

With that problem behind us, we were free to gather our wits and prepare to sell our house. It was a considerable undertaking especially given the fact I had just started teaching in the school. We wanted our home to shine and show its charm for the lookers to want for themselves. So, we went to work.

The yard was first. We threw out the cast-offs that were lying around, so there was nothing left that we were not using. We freshened the flower beds and made sure the lawns were well-watered and mowed. We had good curb appeal, considering the area we were in and the back patio was a pleasant place to sit, sip iced tea and watch the children play. I loved our space and thought it looked fantastic.

The weekend before the real estate agent was going to come to check out our property, we decided to clean our garage. So, out with everything. Down with the cobwebs and out with the dust. We cleared the floor, vacuumed, and mopped, then put everything back as neatly as possible. I put up fresh curtains.

The inside was simple because I had recently painted all the rooms that needed it. All I had to do was filter through the closets for things we no longer needed and make sure they were in order. I just had to keep up with my usual housework, which was more of a challenge these days.

Dan and I were excited because our agent was due to come over the next day. He went to work, and I was home with our four children. Matthew was six, Mark was four, Sarah, three and Luke was just over a year old. Sarah and Luke stayed in the house with me while Matthew and Mark went outside to play in the backyard. I busied myself with housework, etc.

As I was working, I could hear my high-spirited little boys having a marvelous time. After a while their joyful shrieks pushed my concern button. What are those boys up to? A peek out the window confirmed my instincts. They were running around the far back portion of the yard with the hose. This wouldn't have been a big deal, had they not been unabashedly naked.

Boys, enough! I opened the window and ordered them into the house. They just laughed and ignored me. Annoyed, I marched out to retrieve them. On my way, I stopped in my tracks at the sight of what I considered to be a disaster. The two hooligans dug a big pit next to the patio and filled it with water. What fun it must have been prancing and jumping around in the gushy pond, splashing mud up on the side of our house. Oh no! What a terrible mess. There's no way we can fix this by tomorrow.

The boy's feet and legs were covered in mud. I had to spray them off before I could let them into the house, which delighted them even more. As I led them in, I noticed the back garage door was open. Uh oh. I peeked in to see what that was about. To my horror, I saw they found the large bag of wild bird seed we had sitting on the floor. I surveyed the damage. There were seeds spread all over the garage. They must have had a free-for-all party. I could imagine them grabbing handfuls and tossing them into the air. What Fun!

CHAPTER 16

Binding Together

School's opening brought the impending annual seven-day fast. I dreaded what it would be like. The Lord had mercy on us. Much to my relief, Miguel called a twenty-one-day "Daniel fast" instead. We could eat vegetables and legumes. I felt like dancing. It would be grueling but better than starving.

The hardest thing for me to give up was my morning coffee. We couldn't have herbal tea, so I would drink hot water. I could at least have something warm after getting up. It wasn't what I was accustomed to, but I was somewhat appeased. Our children were good sports about the whole thing. I served a lot of beans and various forms of potatoes to fill their bellies.

It wove a sense of camaraderie. We shared recipes and commiserated with one another. Everyone chimed into the countdown of days, and excitement intensified as we approached the end. It was a slow twenty-one days.

Day zero finally came. The whole fellowship met up at a place where there were several orchards open for people to visit, buy apple treats, pick through pumpkin patches, ride on a mini-train, and comb through art and craft fairs.

We joined in worshipping the Lord and praying for a while and then tore into boxes of sumptuous, warm apple donuts to break the fast. The adults sat at picnic tables and chatted while the children ran through the rows of trees.

The years of seven days with just water ended. The Daniel fast became our annual fall tradition. I don't think I was the only one who was joyous over the change.

Early December brought our family some happy news. I remember the day. I was at school preparing to take the first grade on a field trip to the railroad museum, when a phone call came for me.

"Is this Flori Paquette?" the lady from my doctor's office asked. "Yes, it is."

"I'm calling to let you know that your pregnancy test is positive."

"Hallelujah! That's wonderful!"

I hung up and danced in the hallway, announcing my good news to everyone. A familiar glow waved through me. *Yay, I'm going to have another baby!*

Until that day, I was only somewhat familiar with Ms. Annie. We had not worked closely enough to get to know each other. She volunteered to come along on our field trip. While ushering the children through the museum tour, showing them the Wells Fargo stagecoach, and taking turns riding on horse-drawn carriages, it was apparent she loved being with the kids. I found her delightful to talk to. She was someone I could relax with and relate to. It was refreshing and comforting because I found a new friend.

December brought the annual three-day fast and winter retreat. It was a time in the mountains for us to worship and seek the Lord. Everyone in the covenant had to go.

Dan and I stuffed snow clothes, sleeping bags, pillows, towels, and kids into our funky VW van and wound our way along to the remote retreat. Close friends from our church joined us along the way. Our families descended on a restaurant in town to fill our bellies before the misery began.

In crisp mountain air surrounded by pine trees were little cabins spread out on a hillside above the main lodge. Each family had a dusky cabin with two sets of bunk beds and a bathroom. There was a dining hall for the children.

The adults had only water, from Thursday after dinner to Sunday lunch. There was an exception for pregnant and nursing mothers who could eat vegetables and legumes.

Since I was going to have a baby, I could eat with the children. Dan had to fast with everyone else.

The main lodge looked like a single-story brown mountain house. There was a large room with indoor/outdoor carpeting and rows of metal chairs facing a woodburning fireplace with a large stone hearth. Next to it stood an old upright piano. The crackle and glow of the flames warmed the milieu, offering a pleasant contrast to the cold outside.

It was exciting for the children because they could run through the woods and play. When it snowed, they spent their time sledding and making snowmen. The adults met for the mornings and evenings. The meetings could go on indefinitely, often into the early hours of the morning. It wasn't an easy time. We joined to draw close to the Lord and bind together in love. Though there was uplifting worship, the ventures through the Bible led by Miguel and the elders were oppressing. They left me with the feeling that we weren't as dedicated to God as we should be.

The Saturday meetings tended to be more encouraging. The children performed something like a Nativity play and singing. The Bar Mitzvah and Bat Mitzvah ceremonies for the youth who had prepared for it were also on that day. They stood in front of the congregation and recited a chapter of the Bible that they had memorized. It was fascinating to witness. It delighted me to have the children take part in celebrating our Lord. Their pink cheeks and sweet voices reminded me of why we were gathered in the first place.

After the last meeting on Sunday morning, the atmosphere turned jovial as we gathered our children and hiked up the hill to the dining hall. Hallelujah! The fast was over! The bland turkey, potatoes, gravy, and canned vegetables tasted heavenly.

Miguel had all the children squeeze together for a group picture, and then we all marched down to our cabins to pack our belongings and scrub our dwellings from top to bottom. We had to leave them sanitized and cleaned down to the window tracks. Interestingly, Miguel and Sandi departed right after lunch. They assigned the single women to clean their cabin for them.

When it was all over with, and we were heading home, I felt invigorated and relieved. With Christmas festivities a few days away, there was plenty to be excited about.

CHAPTER 17

Christmas

With the retreat behind us, we wound down the mountain toward our last-minute preparations for Christmas. We had to squeeze our to-do list into a few days. I had our traditions as a template to follow as I planned what else I had to do.

Our extended families lived a hundred miles away in opposite directions. Because I spent all my childhood holidays split between my parents, I wanted my children to spend their Christmases at one home. I wanted it to be as stress-free and consistent as possible. Therefore, we made it clear to our families that if they wanted us to be with them during this season, they would have to come to our house.

We never put gifts under the tree until Christmas Eve after the children were asleep. They were always excited, so they weren't tucked into their dreams until very late. Dan and I would have everything hidden, wrapped, and ready to go, and then we went to bed and slept. Around two thirty in the morning, the alarm rang.

With the children oblivious to the world, we made ourselves some fortified eggnog and got to work. With gifts piled around the tree and stockings hanging on the children's dining room chairs, we went back to bed until we could hear the children tittering around.

They could dig into their stockings when they woke up, but the presents under the tree had to wait. When the beds and rooms were in order and Dan and I were present, coffee in hand, the kids dug into their bounty. We opened one gift at a time, so the morning wouldn't be a wild free for all. It also made the specialness last longer.

The children had their own tradition. They worked together to get the table ready for breakfast while Dan and I would still be sleeping. It was a sweet blessing to wake up to a dressed-up table every Christmas morning.

Breakfast waited for us in the kitchen—bacon, Grandma Betsy's cheese eggs, and Aunt June's stolen. There were candy and cookies, nuts and cheeses, and crackers from gift baskets. It was all mouthwatering. The best part was the hot stolen with butter melted into it.

With Christmas carols playing in the background, the youngsters played around the house while Dan and I got down to the business of preparing our dinner. We would have juicy roast beef or ham with all the trimmings and some delectable dessert from our favorite bakery.

Woven through these traditions, we read different versions of the Christmas story and talked about its true meaning. We taught the kids that it was God who was pouring the gifts out to them, and the greatest gift of all is Jesus. However, in my heart, I felt that we were falling short of the true spirit of the season. I carried an undefinable longing for something more penetrating to permeate our souls.

CHAPTER 18

The Descent of the Hook

By the time the new year began, I was feeling the familiar surges of nausea and dragging along in the fatigue of early pregnancy. Despite the joy and anticipation of expecting a baby, there was no pleasure in the way I felt physically.

I dragged myself through the days. I could feel myself slipping. On top of church activities and school, we had to keep our house ready for hopefully interested buyers. Add to this the day-in, day-out necessities like meal planning, grocery shopping with all my children in tow and getting homework done. There were also frequent visits to the doctor. It seemed someone or other needed to see him.

A mean cold took me down. I tried to push my way through it, but one day at school, I hit a wall. I melted on the couch in the teachers' room, hoping that Brad would let me go home. He gave me the rest of the week off. It was a great relief. However, I was too sick to enjoy it. My family needed me to watch over them, and the lessons still had to be completed, which required a lot of homework on my part. My blessed husband did all he could to help. Without him, I couldn't have made it through.

At the end of the week, still feeling a substantial need for more rest, I called Brad to request more time off. He said they needed me at school.

At first, shock numbed me. Then the hook took a slow descent into my gut. My thoughts, feelings, and family situation meant nothing compared with the needs of the school. I thought the Lord was calling me to give up my sense of direction, and He wanted me to be sunnyside up about it as well.

This was difficult for me. I had to pray hard for the strength to go back to school the following Monday. I dragged myself along until the cold left my body, but I still had to push my way through the morning sickness, which, for me, lasted all day and through the night.

I struggled with my disappointment and anger. Being under such stress was detrimental to my family. I wanted to announce "Enough of this. I quit." I knew the Lord understood my feelings but believed He was telling me not to lean on my way of seeing things. "Trust in the Lord with all your heart and lean not on your own understanding; in all your ways acknowledge Him, and He will direct your paths" (Proverbs 3:5–6 [NKJV]).

I was faltering, but Scripture states that His strength is made perfect in our weakness.

I prayed hard for the internal resources my service required. The Lord provided, but I didn't understand why He was calling me to a place where it was taking its toll on my family. I no longer had the time and energy to do things my heart desired with my children. My vision was being buried alive.

Once again, I thought I was being called to lay my life down at the cross. I looked upon wanting to serve my family and longing to pour more of my energy into my home as if they were my flesh. They came from my "self."

After some time and many prayers to lay it at the Lord's feet, I accepted my circumstances to the best of my ability.

"Obey those who rule over you, and be submissive, for they watch out for your souls, as those who must give an account. Let them do so with joy and not with grief, for that would be unprofitable for you" (Hebrews 13:17 [NKJV]).

I had a desire to be happy, so I looked for things to be grateful for. To answer God's calling, I had to believe that it was for the best. I looked at the very well-organized school. I put my mind to how beautiful it was to hear the children singing and praying and how rewarding it was to listen to them read out loud. Thoughts about how much was being accomplished made me believe that I was living out God's purpose for my life. I didn't think I was dying for no good reason.

By the grace of God, I could lift my chin and move forward.

CHAPTER 19

Summer

The Lord had mercy on me. Dan allowed me to hire a sweet lady named Lori to clean our house once a week. All I needed to do was keep things tidied up for potential buyers.

Spring brought relief from my early pregnancy woes, and the baby quickened. The transportation class continued to be a challenging adventure. My downtrodden spirit lifted.

The end of the school year brought relief from most of my out-of-home duties. I felt light and free. It was good to mellow out with the kids and concentrate on preparations for moving. Sweet anticipation for the future lifted me through the summer days.

A lot of lookers had come through our house. There was plenty of positive feedback but no offers. We lowered the price two times to no avail.

We had a problem. Our house had its twin next door. They started out the same, but the other house was showing wear and tear from our neighbors. The first thing to greet our lookers was the young pig they had in their front yard. There was an engine sitting on a big patch of grease in the driveway. All the windows you could see from the street were broken and covered with black plastic. The grass and the broken-down chain-link fence that surrounded it sorely needed attention.

It didn't matter how cute our house was. Who would want to buy it? So we grieved and waited for a blind buyer to come our way.

We got our miracle. Finally, a single guy who worked at the nearby air force base came along and wanted to buy it. We were ecstatic.

Praising Jesus, we searched for a new place. We were hot on the hunt with our real estate agent leading the way. Our goal was to find a location near the street where the elders lived and the kindergarten classroom was. We called the street Candlewick Central. Many of the church's activities went on there. At that time, there were five families.

Finding a house on that street was considered the perfect location. However, I wasn't interested in living in such proximity to leadership. I feared they would intrude on whatever privacy we had left. They could get even deeper into our home life than they already were.

We found a great house about a mile away. When we showed it to Brad, he wasn't enthusiastic. He said to look for a house on Candlewick way. I was angry that he could put our desire aside just because it wasn't right on that street. I wanted to keep our distance.

Dan listened to me blow off my steam. He didn't seem to mind the thought of living in the middle of things. After all, it was a well -kept neighborhood on a quiet street. It would be an ideal place for the children to play with their friends. Objections aside, we gave up the house we wanted.

It wasn't long before a house went on sale. Brad had us check it out. It was just plain ugly, with a terrible floor plan and a minuscule backyard. Thank God, Brad agreed we should wait for something else.

Within days, another one went on the market. This time it thrilled me. I liked it even better than the other one. Twice the size as where we were coming from and directly across the street from the kindergarten, it was perfect. We gave God the glory for opening an ideal place for us to spread our roots.

I was approaching the birth of our fifth child. We were in the crunch to finish our packing and get our new house ready to move in. It was a hectic time. I was paying close attention to my aches, pains, and contractions as we went along. We wondered what would happen first. *Oh, baby, are you going to come on moving day?*

By the grace of God, we had all the help we needed. It was customary for the Tamarisk people to support members when they moved. Brad lined up a crew of people to help get our things transported and moved into our new home. Then there was a team of ladies to help with getting our essentials put away. So they set us up and ready to settle in and make our new house a home.

At the end of moving day, we went to bed exhausted. I lay in bed as we watched our baby move around in my tummy. The sky in my soul was clear except for some clouds of fear that had blown into the distance.

CHAPTER 20

Welcome to Candlewick

My eyes opened on the first day in our new house. I was wrapped in the newness of my surroundings. Warm summer light illuminated the creamy colors of the freshly painted hallway and stairwell. I curled up under the sheets, feeling the baby stirring, until Dan woke up a minute or two later. Giving him a soft nudge, I said, "Hey, we are here in our new house. This is it. We live on Candlewick."

"It's great to have it all over with."

"I'll never forget how hot it was. I felt sorry for all the guys who helped. They looked like they were melting." I pulled myself up, ruffled my pillows for support, and then sat up in bed.

"I'm still pregnant." I pouted.

Dan reached over and put his hand on my belly.

"I can see that, even after the move and everything."

"When is our child going to come? I keep thinking I'm starting labor, but then it quits."

"It will be born when it's ready. Meanwhile, you have plenty to do to keep you busy. You won't have to sit around bored while you wait."

Dan peered at the clock sitting on his nightstand. "Look at what time it is. It's seven thirty. We better start getting ready, or we'll be late."

I took a deep breath and blew it out.

"Oh, I wish we could relax and take it all in. I'm stiff from all the work we did yesterday. Why can't we stay home from church just this once?"

"We can't stay home from church, Flori. You know that would never fly. I'll go make some coffee while you lie there a little longer until we have to get the kids ready to go." Dan headed for the kitchen.

There wasn't a single muscle in my body that wanted to get up just yet— the irritation from not having the option to stay home on this morning burned in my chest. *Here we are tired and surrounded by piles of boxes. We can't break into this day slowly. Why the rush to get out the door?* I took a deep breath, whipped the sheets back, and lifted my cumbersome body out of bed. There was no use letting myself be upset. *It will only make me miserable.*

Eleven days later, I felt the pinch of my first labor pains. I proceeded with our plan to call Mary-Anne, one of the elders' wives, from down the street. She came over, gathered our children, and escorted them to her house, where they would stay until their prearranged babysitters came to pick them up.

My mom had come down from Tahoe to help with the family. As planned, she accompanied us to the hospital. Our friends Naomi and Susan met us when we arrived. I wanted them to be present when the baby was born.

That night, we held our little Elizabeth in our arms for the first time. She was our fifth child. The familiar warmth and wonder of having a newborn came to life. I was fulfilled and serene as I looked at our new baby girl for the first time. I was happy beyond words that we could bring a new little sister home to the rest of the kids.

When we pulled into the driveway with our adorable bundle in tow, Grandma and the children came out of the house to greet us. I bent over so each of them could marvel at her sweet, swollen face and peek at her tiny hands before we all went inside. Elizabeth was a gift to our whole family.

Our voices echoed in the spaciousness of our new house. It was a dream come true. There was room for all of us to spread out. There was a significant change from having our children confined to their yard on a thoroughfare street with a thirty-five-mile-per-hour speed limit to a quiet street with many neighbors we were sharing life with. Our older children could walk out of our front door and walk to their friends' houses. They had the run of the neighborhood and many eyes to oversee their activities. An ideal situation such as knowing all the parents and being likeminded about what influences were acceptable was an enormous blessing.

We were getting acclimated to having an additional little person in our family and our new surroundings when the school year began. Mark's eyes were lit his first morning of kindergarten. He was adorable as he gathered his things and headed out the door. It tickled me to watch his preciousness, while his oversize backpack bounced up and down as he awkwardly skipped across the street. He headed down the sidewalk toward a new grand adventure. Now he got to be like his brother, doing big boy stuff.

I had given birth just a few weeks prior. Therefore, no one expected me to teach. Instead, they assigned me children to watch over while their mother was at school. I liked the situation because I could be at home with my little ones and do housewifely things. We let go of Lori when we moved because we had a higher house payment.

Now we had two boys sitting at the dining room table with their homework spread out before them. They were still young and needed a lot of support from Dan. It amazed me how much homework Mark had each night. Reading, writing, and math five nights a week. They started teaching the kids to read the first day they stepped into the classroom.

Before school started, the teachers met with the fathers to let them know what was expected of them while doing homework with the kids. Dan sat with the boys and went over their homework. He signed each paper and the assignment tag to show that he checked over all the work.

Soon after school began, it was time for the "Daniel fast" again. Another twenty -one days of vegetables and legumes. Though I was nursing Elizabeth, I had to keep the fast along with everyone else. Pregnancy and lactating was not an excuse from what the rest of the fellowship was doing, which didn't bother me a bit. Since I could have peanut butter to spread on my yams, I was good with it.

Moving to Candlewick made our life smoother. We were happy to be living there.

CHAPTER 21

Say What?

Now we lived in Tamarisk's hub. We didn't have our own church building for our midweek activities. Most of the flock gatherings and prayer meetings happened in the elder's homes. Members of our church were always coming and going for various reasons. We were becoming familiar with more of the people in the fellowship because we would bump into them more often than when we lived several miles away.

We were closer to the people who lived under Miguel for many years. Most of them had been with him since they were in junior high school or were young single people when they came under his tutelage. I held these people in awe. They were at the heart of what was going on. Part of me looked up to them. However, it intimidated me to be around them. I was afraid that they would find fault in my family or me and Dan.

One sunny fall afternoon, my doorbell rang. It was one such person. I knew her name was Eleanor but had no close contact with her. She came over to drop some papers off for Dan.

Eleanor was about my age with young children like me. Her demeanor put me at ease. We struck up a friendly exchange about Dan and me and our Blessed Spirit flock. I told her how we met Brad and that he had been our pastor since before we had our third child. Somewhere in our conversation, she said something about Dan and me having problems in our sex life.

My ears could have fallen off the side of my head. It flabbergasted me. Her audacity blew my mind. How could this person think anything of the kind?

"Where on earth did you hear that?"

She said, "Miguel told me." As if it wasn't out of the ordinary.

Miguel? The only thing he could know is from the conversation I had with Brad. I had asked Brad if a woman had to comply with every intimate inclination of her husband.

"You mean to tell me you guys talk about such things amongst each other?"

"Oh, for sure, all the time." She laughed.

"It's impossible to keep a secret around here."

Shocked, I said nothing. I didn't know how to respond to someone so close to Miguel.

Eleanor gave me the papers for Dan. We said a friendly goodbye, and she left.

My head was spinning. *What business did Brad have telling Miguel something I asked him about? Aren't pastors supposed to keep stuff like that confidential?* I plopped myself down on the couch. I sat there, with the little ones playing around me and the older kids running in and out, having fun with their friends. *That's how things work around here? There's no privacy?* I shuddered. The realization of what living in this community would be like squeezed me too tight for comfort.

When Dan came home from work, I poured out what Eleanor had told me.

"You're kidding me. She said what?" Dan put his briefcase down and loosened his tie.

"How did she come up with that?"

"Brad must have said something to Miguel about what I asked him. It's the only way I can think of."

Dan headed upstairs and beckoned me to follow him. We went into our bedroom and shut the door. I sat on the bed while Dan changed into his shorts and a T-shirt.

"I don't see any reason for Brad to talk to Miguel. Aren't pastors supposed to keep people's conversations to themselves?"

"I thought so, but I guess it's different around here." Dan scrunched his face and shook his head as if he just tasted something terrible.

"Then Miguel had the audacity to tell Eleanor about it? There's no reason for that." My eyes followed Dan around the room.

"You're right. That's hard to fathom." He opened the door and headed down the stairs.

It frustrated me. Dan didn't think it was right, but it didn't appear to get under his skin as much as it did me.

The kids were at the bottom of the stairs to greet their father. It was always a big deal to have Dad home from work. We put our conversation on hold while we went through our evening routine. I stayed quiet about how upset I was through dinner, homework, and bath time. When the children were tucked into their beds for the night, I brought the subject up again.

"What should we do about it? Should we confront Brad?" I asked.

Dan was quiet while I went on about how wrong I thought it was. He was not one to share all his thoughts. After letting him have some time to chew on it, I asked again,

"What should we do?"

"I don't want you to say anything. We just have to get used to the way things are."

Though I didn't think what they did was right, I accepted what Dan said. When it came down to it, I was afraid of saying something.

"Well, I guess I'll just have to be very careful about what things I say, or it could spread everywhere."

CHAPTER 22

What's Yours is Mine

We demanded a lot from our old Volkswagen van. Dan's family lived in the Bay Area and mine in Lake Tahoe and Reno. We visited them often, which put a lot of miles on our not-so-reliable transportation. We broke down in the mountains on our way to Reno. It took a hefty chunk of our pocketbook to fix it. We were exasperated. There was no way under heaven we wanted to take it out of town and find ourselves stranded somewhere again. If we wanted to see our families, we had to borrow a van, or they had to come to us.

The Lord poured an enormous blessing on us. Dan's parents bought us a brand-new, twelve-passenger Ford Club Wagon. It was a beauty. It was cream with brown side panels, and seats were covered with a plush velveteen upholstery. As big as it was, it was easy to drive and had a smooth ride. We were all exuberant and very grateful.

We decided on a twelve instead of an eight-passenger van, which would have been enough to carry our family. The school leased a wing of classrooms in an old high school that was converted into a community center. All the students were dropped off on our street, where we carpooled them over to the school. The more seats we had, the more kids we could transport, using fewer cars.

I was still just a babysitter. I didn't need to drive to the school. One teacher used our van to transport the kids. She told me she needed her own set of keys.

It took me back. It bothered me to be told to make her a set. I told her she should come to get the keys from me when she was going to be using our van. She didn't understand, so she went to Miguel. He called and told me I had to make her a set to keep.

The reason made sense. It was so that she didn't have to come up to my door every morning. It was practical. I had no problem letting someone else drive our van for the school. That was why we got a big one. I felt that it was presumptuous of them to treat my van as if it was theirs. If I was asked instead of told, it would have made all the difference.

I had a set of keys made and gave them to the driver. I came away from it feeling like I was viewed as selfish, wanting to withhold my possession from the Lord.

CHAPTER 23

The Departure

During our first year in the neighborhood, Miguel's influence became more pronounced in our life. Brad was still the shepherd of the Blessed Spirit flock, but there was a subtle shift in who was guiding us. Brad was more in the background. Something obscure was happening between the leadership and Brad. Blessed Hope was melting into Tamarisk like butter on toast.

Brad's wife, Susan, came over to my house one spring day. I remember sitting on my bed with her, playing with little Elizabeth. As usual, Susan was her warm, sweet self with glossy pink lips. She opened her Bible and read a passage to me: "Receive one who is weak in faith, but not to disputes about doubtful things. For one believes he may eat all things, but he who is weak eats only vegetables. Let not him who eats despise him who does not eat and let not him who does not eat, judge him who eats; for God has received him" (Romans 14:1–3 [NKJV]).

She said that Miguel was wrong to pressure us to eat a vegan diet as if it was a godlier way to eat. She said that, according to the Bible, we were free to choose, and it did not reflect on how spiritual we were.

I listened to her but had mixed emotions swirling in my gut. My chest tightened. *Oh my god, she's talking against Miguel. That's rebellion, which is as the sin of witchcraft.* It made me sad to think that even though she was right about the way of eating, she was walking on dangerous ground thinking and speaking against our leader.

There was a part of me that wanted to agree with her and listen further, but my guard went up. Brad did a thorough job of convincing us not to take a stand against our designated authority. Susan was clearly speaking in opposition to Miguel.

By the end of the season, they removed Brad from his position as pastor. They never gave us an explanation. It was hush-hush between the elders, so we just accepted it as some disciplinary action. Dan and I assumed it was something we weren't supposed to question. Miguel stood in Brad's place as our immediate shepherd. We were curious about what was going on. However, we figured they would tell us what they wanted us to know. We let it go at that.

One day we were over at Brad and Susan's. Brad came into the kitchen. When he saw us, his eyes brightened, and a smile seemed to reverberate through his whole body. "I have something to tell you." He opened his arms wide. "I understand what's been wrong. It's all coming clear to me now."

I stiffened and caught my breath—fear of what he would say filled my ears with static. I didn't even try to focus on what he was saying because I felt like he would say something contradictory to the things he had convinced us of. Because of his standing with leadership, I thought that whatever he had to say would be rebellious.

Neither Dan nor I gave him a chance to finish what he was saying. We said it was time for us to go.

A few weeks later, Brad and his family left Tamarisk. We had no more contact with them. Miguel never made the details of what happened clear to us. We didn't question it, assuming Brad was hurt because he was told to step down as a pastor.

CHAPTER 24

The Ugly Truth

A month or two after Brad and Susan left the church, Dan was ready to work on fixing up our yard. First, he had to put in a sprinkler system. Miguel took Dan under his wing. He offered to help Dan do some of the work. Dan accepted.

It was a bright autumn afternoon. Miguel was working on digging the trenches in our backyard. I went outside to give him a glass of water. Somehow we ended up in a discussion about being candid about our thoughts and feelings. He was trying to tell me how vital speaking the truth is in the body of Christ. I tried to tell him that there are times we shouldn't speak out our critical thoughts. He was adamant that we should.

An example thought popped into my head. It made me cringe with how awful it was. It was straight out of the depravity of my soul. There was no way I wanted to speak it.

I argued with Miguel.

"But the Bible says there is a time to speak and a time to be quiet." Miguel managed, in his usual way, to confound me with his point of view. He said something about the need to confess our sins.

Frustrated with our conversation, I went back into the house. As I sat up in my bedroom, guilty feelings went through me like waves of nausea. There was no way on God's green earth I wanted to confess my thought. My way of dealing with thoughts like that was to rebuke them in the name of Jesus. I would push them out of my mind.

However, Miguel's words echoed in my head. I thought the Lord was telling me that I had to confess. I fought it but felt I had to obey what Miguel told me to do. I squirmed and hesitated from how humiliated I was.

The burning in my gut got so intense; I was compelled to go downstairs, back out to our dug-up lawn, and approach Miguel. He stuck his shovel next to where he was working and took his gloves off.

"Well, what's up?" he asked, smiling.

"I had a critical thought about someone."

"Yes? And what might that be?"

The words caught in my throat and then stopped behind my teeth. I swallowed and then pushed out.

"I had the thought that Cynthia is ugly."

I could feel the heat of shame and embarrassment rush from my shoulders up through my face, but it was out. My burning guilt and fear could go away.

Miguel slid his hands into his gloves.

"You are going to have to confess that to Cynthia."

I lost my breath. I couldn't believe what I had just heard.

"No way. That can't be right! That would only hurt her," I argued.

"She needs to hear it when you can say it in a loving way." Miguel picked up his shovel and started digging.

"If you wait, it might brew inside of you and come out someday in anger."

I wound up on my bed in tears, hugging my pillow in a fetal position. I couldn't fathom how it was the right thing to do. The thought of it made me roll around, pleading,

"Why God, why?"

Later that afternoon, the phone rang. It was Miguel.

"Have you confessed to Cynthia yet?"

"No, I feel terrible, and I think it's cruel."

"Well, I advise you to take care of it as soon as possible."

I was in my room, agonizing over how I was going to bring myself to tell her, when there was a knock at our front door. It was Jerry, the elder who lived across the street from us.

"I came to take you over to Cynthia's house so you can talk to her." He smiled and had his unique-to-Jerry twinkle in his eye.

It would have been better to face the gallows. Everything inside me wanted to evaporate. Jerry drove me over to Cynthia's house. I stared at her front door. I did not want to knock. Jerry smiled, raised his eyebrows, and waited.

Cynthia's husband let us into the living room and summoned her. I was tight inside and a kind of nervous I find difficult to describe. She gestured for me to sit down.

"I have something terrible that I thought I need to confess."

I'm sure my squirming and fidgeting were obvious and revealed how difficult this was for me.

Cynthia laughed like a little song.

"It's going to be fine, Flori. Go ahead and tell me." Her voice was sweet and gentle.

I sat there, feeling like a cockroach caught in the light.

"I'm so sorry, Cynthia, but I had a critical thought about you."

"Go ahead, honey, you can tell me." She brushed her lap with her hands.

"I had the thought that you were ugly." I shriveled.

"Oh, that's OK. It's not the end of the world."

I poured out the apologies and said how rotten I felt that something like that came through my mind. I told her that she was a truly beautiful person.

Cynthia laughed consolingly. "Oh, don't worry about it anymore. I forgive you. I've been told I resemble Big Bird."

Her countenance made me feel as though she was genuinely merciful toward me. She behaved as though there was nothing shocking or unusual about me having to come to her. Miguel had been her pastor for many years.

Jerry drove me home. I felt relieved and terrible at the same time. It left me with a sickening fear of my own mind. The Lord only knew what kinds of ungodly things could run through my head. Then I would be compelled to confess my shameful thoughts.

That night I lay in my bed and prayed, "Dear God, please be with Cynthia. Cover her when she thinks of what I told her today. Somehow, Lord, soften the blow and help her to not recall this. Dear Jesus, forgive me for being so ugly and shallow. Help me never to think of anyone in this way ever again. All I want to see is the beauty in Your diverse creation. In Jesus's name, Amen."

CHAPTER 25

Symbol of Authority

"But every woman who prays or prophesies with her head uncovered dishonors her head, for that is one and the same as if her head were shaved. For if a woman is not covered, let her also be shorn. But if it is shameful for a woman to be shorn or shaved, let her be covered. For a man indeed ought not to cover his head, since he is the image and glory of God; but woman is the glory of man. Nor was man created for the woman, but woman for the man. For this reason the woman ought to have *a symbol of* authority on *her* head, because of the angels" (1 Corinthians 11:5–10 [NKJV]).

One thing that made Tamarisk unique is that this scripture was interpreted literally. Women had to have heads covered for all the worship and prayer meetings. I often wondered how we looked to other people when we were coming in and out of church or gatherings in our neighborhood such as Bible studies or baptisms. It was a common assumption that the rest of the people on our street thought we were a cult. But of course, we knew better.

I was happy to wear my veil. It made me feel closer to the Amish people I so admired. Their women had to have their heads covered all the time.

After my dreadful confession, I was inundated with guilty feelings over any critical thought that caught my attention. I expressed to Dan my terror of having to confess them to those who were my unfortunate victims.

Dan came home from Miguel's house one day and told me he talked to him about my anxiety. He said Miguel was frustrated with me. Then to my immense relief …

"Miguel said that you are to confess your thoughts to me, and I decide if you need to say something."

"You mean it? For real? If I tell you, that's enough?" My spirit lit up.

"Yes, Flori, that's all you need to do. It's for me to forgive you."

"Thank God!" My heart relaxed, and a warm feeling spread where a terrible tension used to be. I knew I would be safer under Dan's discretion than Miguel's. He would never make me do such a horrible thing to someone. Ever.

I was thoroughly grateful to God that Dan was my husband. The covering I wore on my head took on an even greater meaning to me. It represented Dan's headship and protection.

Still, I had to confess the garbage that entered my thought processes. Poor Dan had to hear about every thought that brought up guilt for me. Something would pop into my head, and I would burn with dread over the idea of having to tell Dan. Then just like when I confessed to Miguel, it sat behind my lips until it built up enough painful steam for me to whistle it out. I went through this through the rest of the Tamarisk years.

At first, I was good at this. My guilt dissipated, and I would go on my happy way. But after going through it several times, I began to fear that God was going to judge Dan because he was so much easier on me than Miguel would be. I observed how others in the fellowship would confess things to one another. They were far more open than Dan would direct me to be.

I worried that God would judge Dan because he wasn't following Miguel's example. My distress grew into full- blown anxiety. I expressed my fear to Dan. He told me not to worry about it. Too bad that didn't ease my mind. I learned to live with a continuous dread, just waiting for God to drop His gavel. I was terrified He would remove Dan from standing in His way. He might not actually kill him off at first, but maybe he would hurt Dan to warn him. I feared that if Dan didn't listen to God's punishments, He would put some sort of curse on him and then possibly remove him from being my cover.

I couldn't function in a constant state of such anxiety, so I pushed it from my awareness. It would pop up in me again every time Dan released me from something. It became a vicious cycle of relief and then fear for Dan's well- being.

When I pinned the veil on my hair, I didn't do it only because I was told to. I wanted it there. It stood for something that was my lifeline. It represented my protection from the kind of things Miguel would have me do.

My heart went out to the women who experienced getting their cover pulled. It was a form of discipline for insubordination. She couldn't wear her head covering. The purpose was to publicly humiliate her and leave her open to Satan for the destruction of her flesh. She would remain that way until the elders believed she repented.

CHAPTER 26

Kindergarten

Along with the heat of late summer in 1990 came preparations for the coming school year. Sandi, Miguel's wife and the current principal of our school, arranged for a few of us women to attend some training on how to teach reading to kindergartners. She also gave me a copy of the book *Math Their Way*, which was the method that we used to introduce the children to beginning math skills. Sandy also recruited me to help with the annual preschool testing.

It was an exciting day for all the pink-cheeked, shiny-nosed little ones and a momentous occasion for those of us who would teach them. I have fond memories of sitting with the eager children, listening to them recite their alphabet and show me how they counted their numbers. I had them write their names and tell me their parents' names and where they lived. Then they went to other teachers to check what colors and shapes they knew and how physically coordinated they were.

Parents were supposed to work with their children during their preschool years. If a little one didn't perform up to the expectations, their mother would be shamed for not spending enough time helping them learn.

Ms. Mary-Anne was the head kindergarten teacher. She was my on-site guide while I learned how to teach the reading, math, and PE programs. An elder's wife and one of the longstanding Tamarisk members, she was "in authority" over me.

She intimidated me because of a day when Luke sneaked out of the house and wandered down the street to her house. She brought him back home, opened the front door, came into our entryway, and gave him a swat with her rod. I stood shocked at the top of the stairs, horrified by what she had the audacity to do. I thought she should have brought him home, told me about what he did, and left him in my hands to decide if he needed "a correction." However, because she was one of the members for many years and an elder's wife, I didn't dare to stand up against what she did.

I cowered beneath her authoritative demeanor. I was tense as I moved about the classroom under her watchful eye. Being new to her class, I felt like she was paying close critical attention to everything I did. It was like working under a gray shadow.

Other than that, the school year was off to a good start. Matthew went into the third grade, Mark into first. Sarah was in kindergarten. She was in my reading and math groups. It delighted me that I could be one of her teachers.

I had fun teaching the kids but was also feeling the strain of being very busy at home. We couldn't afford to have household help because we had a higher house payment. I was on my own with the housecleaning. On top of that, Elizabeth was still in cloth diapers. It was a challenge to keep up with all my responsibilities.

CHAPTER 27

Grace

School was back in session a few weeks when I found out I was pregnant again. Just as the other times, Dan and I were happy. It was a blessing from heaven. I had a strong feeling that it was another baby girl. Of course, we had no way of knowing, but the name Grace kept floating through my mind.

One afternoon, I was angry at Dan for some long-forgotten reason. However, I do remember stomping down the stairs, speaking out my feelings in a voice that demanded attention. When I reached the foot of the stairs, I saw Miguel in the entryway with Dan.

Miguel stopped me in my tracks.

"Hey, you better get a grip on that anger, or you will kill that baby you are carrying."

Rolling my eyes.

"Oh, come on, that's not true."

Miguel pointed his finger at my chest.

"I'm telling you, Flori, anger like that can snuff the life out of an unborn child." He said in his bold, self- assured manner.

I didn't bother arguing. He went back to his discussion with Dan. I walked into the family room. *That's ridiculous. Emotions don't kill babies. Do they?*

For Thanksgiving, we packed our brood and went to spend time with Dan's family in Sunnyvale. It was delightful to be around them. The children loved every opportunity to be with them. I didn't do much to help that year. Morning sickness waylaid me onto the couch to watch the festivities. Dan's sister, Susan, went from person to person, asking them what Thanksgiving meant. The children were adorable to watch. Their answers reflected all that they were learning.

Right after school let out for Christmas break. Preparation for the winter retreat up at Harding Crest began. I had to get as ready for Christmas as I possibly could and then pack everyone for several days away from home. I was relieved that my nausea was easing up and my energy returning. It made getting ready less burdensome.

Up the hill, we went. I was happy to be pregnant because I didn't have to go for three days with only water. My poor honey, being a man, had to fast.

I dreaded the gatherings in the main hall. As in regular covenant meetings, the adults got together to worship, pray, and discuss community issues. Members may find themselves "on the hot seat" for some perceived sin that came to leadership's attention. Such confrontations could be lengthy. Members could take turns questioning and reprimanding them. It was very rare for anyone to stand in defense of the individual. That could be like charging solo out on a battlefield.

One meeting, during fellowship prayer, an elder stood and announced that he sensed the spirit of death in the room. A shock went through me. It left me with a scary, dreadful sensation. The thought of it sickened me. *I hope it's all in his imagination. Don't dwell on it.* I tried to put it out of my mind, but I couldn't thoroughly shake the feeling that someone could die.

Christmas came and went. My father, stepmother, and half sister came to visit us over the New Year. I was excited because though they wouldn't come to church with us, they met people in our fellowship and spent time having fun with them.

Every New Year's Day, our church gathered in our neighborhood for a parade. The children decorated their bicycles and tricycles with crepe paper and balloons. That year, a boy showed up with his bike converted into an airplane float. The adults walked alongside the kids as they circled the block. It was one of the special things we did together.

After the parade, we had our annual progressive dinner. Several of the Candlewick homes would be open with food shared by all. I was elated. Everyone was hospitable toward my family. I wanted them to see we were involved with good people who loved the Lord.

I was glad to be back into my maternity clothes. My tummy didn't have to bear the squeeze of tight-waisted pants. I had entered the easy part of pregnancy.

The next day, we returned to school. Before leaving the house, I made a last-minute trip to the bathroom. I was shocked to find a hint of blood. I only had a few minutes to gather my things and get over to the kindergarten classroom. Since it was too early to call the doctor, reaching her had to wait.

I worried my way through the reading and math lessons. Then when I had a break, I called Dr. Adams. The women in our fellowship called her by her first name, Marilee. She told me to see her in the afternoon.

Dan joined me at the doctor's office. I lay on the table looking up at the screen while Marilee did a sonogram to check on the baby.

"Oh my god!"

My heart fell off a cliff and landed on the frozen ground of a terrible, unfixable reality. There would be no sweet-smelling newborn, no baby brother or sister for the children. Pain sliced through me that I didn't know how to handle. It altered my world.

Marilee told us to go home to wait for labor to start. There was no way to know how long I would have to wait, carrying a dead baby inside me. I was horrified that I was going to have to go through such a horrible thing at home without her. It was a powerful reminder of the sorrow Susan went through when she had to face giving birth to her dead son.

I dragged my broken spirit through the following day. We occupied it with tears and phone calls to tell people our sad news.

That night, after crying myself to sleep, I awakened to some hard cramping that felt like mid- labor. It wasn't long before I felt like I needed to head for the bathroom. I barely got there when I was overwhelmed with heavy bleeding. My strength and balance left me, so I fell to the floor. Every time I tried to lift myself, I felt a rush of blood.

Dan tried to lift me but didn't have enough room to get a solid hold of me. When I tried to help him in the effort, more blood came out. I felt completely out of control and couldn't stop shaking.

"What do you want me to do?" Dan was desperate.

"Call Polly!" I yelled. She was our fellowship's RN who lived around the corner.

"No."

"Why not?" I said in a louder, higher-pitched yell.

"I don't want to wake her."

"Then call Miguel!" I screamed.

Before I knew it, Miguel, the want-to-be paramedic, was at my side. He was well versed in first aid, so he took charge of the situation. He padded my bottom with sanitary napkins and used duct tape to secure them in place. After that, he and Dan carried me downstairs and laid me in the car. Dan sped to the hospital, where they rushed me into an examination room.

I screamed from the physical and emotional pain that roared like a violent sea.

The nurse wouldn't let Dan stay with me. When I begged her to let him, she escorted him through the door.

Marilee was already at the hospital, so it wasn't long before she was at my side. She asked where Dan was. When she heard what happened, she told the nurse to get him. In the midst of all the trauma, I breathed a grateful sigh. I felt calmer with my honey next to me and sweet Marilee in control.

The doctor delivered our baby girl. She gave her to us so we could see her and spend time with her. She was wholly formed with little eyes, nose, ears, fingers, and toes. She stared into space with pale blue eyes. She was lifeless.

After Marilee gently took our tiny girl away, a nun came in to see us. She asked if we wanted her to see to it that the baby was buried. Her offer blessed me. She was being treated like the little person she was instead of like "products of conception," like aborted babies.

The nun was warm and kind. She asked us if we had a name for our baby girl.

"I think her name should be the one that we've been talking about," I whispered to Dan.

"Her name is Grace," Dan told the nun.

CHAPTER 28

Why?

I could barely walk, but they discharged me anyway. When we got home, Dan helped me lift my broken heart and drained body upstairs, where he put me to bed. Sleep came easy.

Waking was hard. Reality felt cruel. I didn't want to face the path that lay before me, but the children's voices beckoned me forward. They knew that we lost our baby, but they weren't as deeply affected as Dan and me were.

Miguel had been kind enough to wipe the floor, but the carpet still needed to be shampooed. I made my way down the stairs, into the laundry room, where I found all the towels that Miguel had used. To add to the whole loss, I had the mess to clean up. I was still too drained to take on the project, so I managed my way back to bed while Dan took care of the kids and got the older ones off to school.

When I got up again, I was dizzy and felt void of all strength. I collapsed on the floor. Life seemed too big for me to carry. Dan got me back in bed and called the doctor. She admitted me to the hospital to give me some intravenous fluids and rest.

It was a bittersweet stay. Another nun came to see me. She listened to me pour my heart out. She was tenderhearted and supportive. There was a rose on my meal tray. I felt like everyone there understood that it was a terrible loss for me.

While I was in the hospital, I waited for Miguel to come see me or call me. I was deeply hurt that I didn't hear from him. I thought he cared about what I was going through, and I thought he would want to check on me.

A few days later, when I was at home, I finally spoke with Miguel on the phone. I expected to receive some words of comfort, which he had for me, but I wasn't expecting what else he had to say.

"I know it's tragic for you to lose your baby, but you realize that it happened because of your anger."

I swooned. It was a good thing I was sitting down when he said it. It was a sickening shock.

"What? No! Anger can't kill babies," I argued.

"Pregnant women go through all kinds of intense feelings, and their babies are born just fine."

"I'm sorry to have to tell you this, but it is your toxic anger that took your baby's life."

"Are you telling me I killed the baby inside of me?" I didn't want to accept what he was telling me, but he was so self-assured.

"Well, it wasn't murder. I know you didn't want to. It was more like manslaughter."

Then he told me he was giving me six weeks off to recover, which, at that point, I felt like I would need to get some equilibrium back into my life. Miguel's words took my hollow pain and turned it into irreconcilable grief. It was one terrible thing to have to face the loss, but to deal with being at fault for it was a torment that threw me into a spiritually confused mess.

⚮

Dan seemed to take our situation in stride. "I don't think Miguel is on base about this. Don't take it to heart."

"But then why would he say it?"

"I don't know. Don't worry about it. This kind of thing happens a lot. Something was probably wrong with the baby, and this is God's way of taking care of it. I know it hurts, but it's not something you need to blame yourself for."

Dan seemed low in spirits for a few weeks, but life picked him up and carried him forward. He was busy with a brood of kids, and he was working as a new partner in his accounting firm. If that wasn't enough, it was tax season. He had plenty to keep him occupied.

"There will be other babies. We'll try again when you are feeling better."

I knew miscarriages happened every day. It was a fact of life. Others could mourn their loss and get past it without having to carry the thought that they caused it to happen. That would make it easier to process.

Even though Dan and my mother didn't agree with Miguel's opinion, I couldn't shake what he had to say. I didn't want to believe him, but he knew the scriptures far better than they did, and they weren't a pastor. And I was guilty of being angry.

When my time of recovery ended, my body and mind were ready to face the rest of my life, but my spirit was still suffering the aftershocks. It was like living with a bad back except it was my heart that was hurting me at every turn.

I stood in front of my bedroom mirror looking at the image of someone confused and discouraged. *I'm so weary having to live this way, with our family being under all the pressure it takes to keep the school going. Oh, woman, look at yourself. You better do something with that face of yours.* I picked the concealer and started applying it under my eyes. *Don't forget the blush.*

CHAPTER 29

Turn, Run

Dear Heavenly Father, did I really do this to my baby? Is it my fault? Is it because I want out of this way of living? Is it because I hate all the pressure and not being able to make my life how I want to live and raise my family? O, God, help me understand.

I vacillated between believing Miguel and my desire to go the way of the world and say it was not because of my sin. It sure was tempting.

On one cold, rainy night, somewhere in the middle of winter, I found myself with some time alone. It was a perfect time to sit in the warm light of the fire, letting my thoughts break through the hard crust of my to-do list. My sadness made its way through my pen. I spilled my dying vision of how I wanted our life to be across the lines of my binder paper. I laid out all the things I was losing to the life I was being forced to live. My tears fell on the pages as I wrote.

My life was being taken over to fulfill someone else's vision. Every time I turned around, it seemed God was telling me, "No, you can't live as you see fit."

The pressure to do all the things I was being called to do was turning me into an angry woman. Demands being put on my children to perform like perfect little soldiers were gaining control of my responses to them. There was no time to approach life in an easygoing way. I hated the strict, controlling mother I was but didn't have the space to be easy on my kids. We were caught in a vicious whirlwind caused by someone else's ideas.

I wanted to serve God, but I was struggling with having to lay my life down to what I was told. *Is this the anger that killed my baby? I'm fighting God. Is this a punishment or a consequence?*

I grabbed my paper, wrinkled it into a ball, threw it in the fire, and watched the flames turn it into ash. Tears poured down my neck as the fire died down to embers.

The pain had to find a way of expression. I picked up my pen and wrote:

Turn, Run

From the beating of the drum Make my body become numb
Block it out Cover my ears
So I will not feel the tears
Run, Run Stay far away
Move on, press on, another day
Don't listen Don't dance
Don't let my heart romance
Keep my eyes away Can't bear to look
For what I see, I may not be

There is no room There is no time

The truth within me is a crime

I must conform I cannot be

That person who is really me

I write it out My heart's desire

Then turn and burn it up with fire

There is no use It's not the pace

So throw it in the fireplace

Long after the ashes Have grown cold

I feel my heart grow sad and old

Live the other life I see The one I force And learn to be

Dance I must

To someone else's song Why is mine so very wrong?

My body, my energy Is what is needed

My heart, I fear, will not be heeded

Not as smart is what I fear So I go on and play the part

Ignore the pounding of my heart

I know how

To make myself be Almost anything, then call it me

What is your wish?

What is your pleasure?

I'll give it to you in full measure.

I hide the truth Can't let you in

I'm so afraid you'll call me "sin."

That's rejection I can't face

So I keep trying to run the race.

The anger's been raging Long and hot

Be myself; I must not.

I don't fit I can see

There is no room for the real me.

I've been hurting For so long
Because I cannot sing my song.
My fear, my grief, my anger Made my womb
A place of doom.
I tried to toss my heart away But had to face it
On that day.
My baby's death Cut me open wide
So the truth I could not hide.
And now dear God Where to from here?
I must now conquer all this fear.

CHAPTER 30

Lay it Down, Lady

In a cry for help, I gave Miguel a copy of my poem. He wanted me to read it the following Sunday. It felt good that he thought it was something everyone should hear.

I tried to keep my voice from trembling. *Read slow and steady.* I pushed the words out toward all the faces staring at me. *What will they think about what I'm telling them? How will they judge me?*

When service was over, several people said they could identify with what I wrote. I was surprised Miguel's secretary say she understood what I was feeling. *You mean I'm not the only one? Even someone who seems to be one of the most dedicated struggles also?*

I left the church with peace because there were others who were experiencing similar frustrations. I wondered if Miguel wanted me to share because he thought it would be a catalyst for change. It gave me some hope that somehow the injustice would be exposed and worked through.

My hope lifted with the following sunrises but faded with the passing sunsets.

I could accept my loss of our baby, though Miguel's gripping words continued to twist and turn in my mind. It haunted my thoughts at night after I went to bed.

During the day, I couldn't ruminate over it. The alarm rang early in the morning. Time to wake the kidlings and get them breakfast. We had the older children make sandwiches and bag them with their snacks. Other Tamarisk children came over and would wait while we were rushing through our last-minute routine. The kids would fill our van. Another mother would drive them to school.

I walked across the street to the kindergarten classroom where I spent the morning. Two teachers taught reading and math. After that, it was time for lunch and then PE, my final subject of the day. Cynthia had the children for art.

Teaching reading was rewarding. Math fascinated me. Everything was hands-on. We sorted different objects. Pattern making and exploring the various math concepts using manipulatives and games were fun for me and the children.

Although instructing the children was fulfilling, being forced to give my time and energy away from home continued to frustrate me. I had to give up doing things I loved with my family. I went from baking our bread from scratch and sewing my kids' pajamas to rushing through the grocery store to grab quick-fix dinners. All I could do with my sewing machine was dust its cover.

I spent hours helping my children with their homework but had little energy to sit curled up on the sofa and read classic stories to them. I wanted to put more into being a homemaker and mommy. School and church activities threw me off balance.

My calendar was always full. Errands filled most afternoons. I recall writing lesson plans and helping with homework in waiting rooms. Many times I had to bring other peoples' kids with us because I was babysitting.

Evenings were full. I cooked dinner and made sure everyone got their bath. Dan checked over and signed pages of homework. Many nights, the books were open until bedtime.

Once the children were asleep, I would crawl into my feather bed drained. That was my time to read my Bible, pray, and let myself lay in His arms. My feelings would float to the surface, and I would ponder the questions I had simmering on my back burner.

I was struggling over dying to myself to follow Jesus. "Most assuredly, I say to you, unless a grain of wheat falls into the ground and dies, it remains alone; but if it dies, it produces much grain. He who loves his life will lose it, and he who hates his life in this world will keep it for eternal life" (John 12:24–25 [NKJV]).

I grappled to accept that God was calling me to lay down what I felt was right because He had a better plan. A scripture kept running through my mind: "There is a way that seems right to a man, but its end is the way of death" (Proverbs 14:12 [NKJV]). I wondered how it applied to my situation.

CHAPTER 31

Bodega Adventure

Community life continued. The end of the school year brought another trip to Bodega Bay with our fellowship. Dan and I bought a king-size, two-room tent to accommodate our brood. It was like the Taj Mahal of tents. We packed our food, bedding, and clothes to be sure we had what we would need if it were cold or warm and sunny.

Despite our efforts to get there early enough to set up camp before dinner, we arrived just before it got dark. First, we pitched our camping castle. It was windy and cold, so we set up Elizabeth's porta crib in the tent and put her in it to keep her safe and out of the cold. We enlisted the older children's semi-help and got to work setting up camp.

The wind was blowing hard. While we were working, it lifted our tent, pulled its stakes out of the ground, and flipped it over, porta bed, toddler, and all. Elizabeth was screaming. We ran and found the bed turned on its side with our little girl frightened but unhurt.

By the time we re- pitched the tent and unpacked, it was dark. Then it was time to fix dinner. Our friends in the next camp over had mercy on us. They were finished with their meal and offered their leftover stew to us. It was perfect. We could eat without going through meal production. We gladly accepted their generosity.

The next morning, I went over to return their pot. Monique greeted me with her bright smile.

"Did you guys get settled in OK?"

"Yes, we are all set up now. Thank you so much for helping us with dinner.

We wouldn't have been able to eat and get to bed until after ten o'clock."

"You are very welcome. It just so happened we had enough leftover."

"Yes, and it was good too. We enjoyed it." I handed the pot to her.

"Oh great, we have our pot back. We missed it last night."

"I'm sorry I didn't return it sooner. I didn't realize you wanted it."

"Oh." She laughed.

"That's OK. We got by without it."

"What?" I was confused. I thought they were finished using it last night.

"It's our pee pot," she said casually.

"We use it when we have to go to the bathroom in the middle of the night."

CHAPTER 32

Vacation

We came from camping in the damp sand, fog, and wind. Dan and the boys cleaned the tent and other equipment. I made sure everything washable was clean, folded, and put away. The kids busied themselves doing things like hiding a frozen pizza on the roof where it could cook in the hot sun. They were creative and rambunctious with their pursuit of entertainment.

Then there was a pleasant week of no phone calls regarding school, we packed for our summer escape. I set about gathering outfits with all the trimmings for each of the children. Then came the swimsuits, towels, and all the beach paraphernalia we had in our possession.

We stuffed it inside and on top of our van then drove off "Candlewick Central." Leaving the street for two weeks off the merry-go-round was like feeling the sun break through the clouds on a chilly day. So we drove on the windy, forest-lined road to Grandma Cathy's in Lake Tahoe. I could feel the tension in my chest gradually dissipate. My mother's house was our home away from home. It's where we went to get away from the hubbub around the Tamarisk tree.

We were the fortunate ones with another place we could run to getaway. Miguel was big on families, so nothing was said about our frequent trips out of town to visit our relatives. I wondered why because everything else about our fellowship was tight. It was one way I reasoned we were not in a cult.

Tahoe was as relaxing as a bunch of kids, two parents, and one very challenging grandma in a tiny, three- bedroom house could be. It was a piece of heaven compared to home.

After Grandma went to work for the day, we packed a big lunch, gathered all our gear, and descended on the beach near our house. There we would set up our cabana, chairs, and blankets. The older kids would hit the water with their raft while the younger ones played with their toys in the sand. Dan and I sat in our chairs, letting the sun bake us. Dan buried himself in a book, and I watched over the children.

Many afternoons, a few clouds would turn into a dark sky. Thunder resounded. That was our signal to cart our things off the beach and head back to Grandma's.

One day we went through our routine and set up. The pine trees swayed. The people on the beach kept their hands on their floating devices so they wouldn't blow away. Then, a strong gust came up. Dan and I watched our cabana get yanked up by the stakes. We jumped out of our chairs, attempting to grab onto it, but before we could, it went tumbling down the beach, stakes and all. I'm sure Dan and I were adorable, jiggling along as we ran by panicking people in our bathing suits, screaming, "Watch out!" We finally caught up with the darn thing, dismantled it, and dragged it back to our site.

While on vacation, we didn't get away from the strict, authoritarian way we were supposed to "discipline" our kids. When a child disobeyed, wack, they would get it on the backside. Though there was some wiggle room for being young, we ran a tight program. I mainly was the one who kept the kids organized, so I was the toughest on them. When Dan was present, he took care of the corrections.

A dark cloud hovered every time we had to pack to go home. I loved Tahoe. My heart wanted to grab onto a tree and never let go. Anticipation of the inevitable pressure was something that sat like wet sand in the pit of my stomach.

As soon as we arrived home, the phone started ringing. Plans and preparations for the coming school year began. There was an extensive list of meetings, lesson plans to write, and supplies to gather.

Each child had to have their uniforms ready. Every year we held a uniform swap so those outgrown could go to other children. Still, we had to order new pieces before the term began.

Miguel was extremely picky about how the children dressed for school. The colors had to be red, white, blue, and khaki. The girls had to wear uniform skirts, no matter how frigid the weather. No fancy ribbons or clips could be in their hair, and they had to wear their red ties a certain way. The boys wore khaki pants or shorts with a white polo top. All the shoes had to be white.

One year, Miguel made a rule that the shoes had to be pure white. They couldn't have any colored logos. That included no silver. When someone happened to have a color on their shoes, they had to replace them. We shopped in three cities before we found a brand that followed the mandate. The whole thing added a lot of nerve-racking tension to an already stressful situation.

Added to the long list of supplies we had to gather, we labeled everything with the kids' names, including every pencil, crayon, etc. In addition, all books had to be covered with brown paper.

Even though classes hadn't started yet, it seemed like summer break ended after we returned home. Dan and I had to make up for the times others handled our cleaning the classrooms and mowing the elders' lawns. We also had to make up for the days we missed out on our turn in the nursery. The only things that made the last part of the summer vacation were, I didn't have to get up at five-thirty in the morning, and the kids only had to keep up with their summer reading lists.

CHAPTER 33

Joy

The following September, I was pregnant again. Fear shackled my happiness. I wondered if the anger that killed Grace still had a grip on me. I tried to squelch any rebellious thoughts. I suffocated feelings that they took my life captive. The church was directing me away from my visions. I repeatedly had to "repent." When I felt frustrated, I thought it was because I was fighting God's will for my life.

When I found out I was pregnant, I felt the baby's name should be Joy. That would bloom in me if everything turned out well. Hope filled me like a hot-air balloon. However, there was thunder rumbling in the horizon of my heart. I feared lightning would strike, and my baby would fall to the ground.

About nine weeks along, I had some spotting. My heart sank. The doctor fit me in that day for a sonogram—no heartbeat. Marilee scheduled me for a D&C the following day. It was supposed to prevent another episode like the last miscarriage.

Even though I wasn't as far along as I was when I lost Grace, discouragement crushed my spirit. When we got home from seeing the doctor, I saw Miguel standing in front of his house. I walked to meet him and tell him my bad news.

"Miguel, I'm losing this baby. Marilee couldn't see a heartbeat."

He looked disappointed. Shaking his head, he said, "Haven't you learned yet?"

It brought back all the grief of my first loss and added another second blow. Losing another baby was devastating enough, but being told I was responsible for it compounded the weight beyond what I could handle. I fell into a depression so deep I couldn't think straight. It seemed impossible to accomplish anything beyond simple tasks. I could barely face the basics of motherhood.

I had my D&C on a Thursday. I was off school the following Friday. The next week was a three-day week because of the approaching Thanksgiving break. I made the mistake of assuming they would give me through the holiday to get my head and body cleared enough to focus on teaching.

It upset Mary -Anne to find out what I was thinking. I called Miguel to see if I was supposed to go back the next week. He said to take off through Christmas. That sounded like more than enough time. However, I was relieved and grateful for his gracious understanding.

I called Rebecca, a woman who had miscarriages in the past. When I lost Grace, she was a sympathetic shoulder I could cry on. Miguel had told her the same thing. She was very understanding about what I was going through. She helped me not feel so alone in my grief.

I picked up the phone.

"Hello, Rebecca? I was wondering if we could get together to talk."

"Why are you calling me?"

Her words stunned me. I wasn't expecting her to sound so blunt.

"I just need to talk to someone who knows what I'm going through."

"Sure, we can get together, but I don't know what it is you want from me."

"I just want to talk, that's all."

We set a time to meet and have coffee.

I poured my heart out to her as we sat in the restaurant. She seemed aloof and didn't say much. I felt hurt that she wasn't as warm or compassionate as she was with my first miscarriage. *What? Why does she seem so cold toward me?*

When we got into the car to go back to my house, she turned to me. "If you've come to me to coddle you, you've come to the wrong person."

It was as if someone punched me in the chest.

"So you've had a miscarriage. Get up and move on."

She turned her body to face me, resting her arm over the top of her steering wheel. "And don't go running to Marilee to ask for support. Don't go looking for her to sympathize with you."

I cannot remember how I responded to her. All I recall is emotion swirling me into a state of nauseating shock. *What have I done that she would be so harsh with me? What's wrong with looking to Marilee for understanding?*

I was struggling before I met with Rebecca, but after her words, the hurt and grief I was going through reduced me to crawling into the back corner of my closet, underneath my hanging clothes. There, I tried to hide from something dark and oppressive that wanted to attack and swallow me. It was an overwhelming force I was far too weak to deal with on my own. *Dear God, please come and rescue me. Please, dear Father, send me some help. I need someone wise and strong who understands.* Even though He seemed silent, I sensed His love for me.

Sitting on my shoes, protected by my nightgowns and robe, I pressed myself against the back wall and curled up in a tight ball. I felt myself floating as if I were in a bubble where insanity could carry me to an imaginary safe place. I was in another dimension. I crawled onto God's lap, where I felt comforted by His heartbeat.

⁂

"Mom? Where are you?" A sweet voice brought me back to where a forbidding spirit lay in wait to suffocate me.

I wanted to stay in my newfound place but didn't want to leave my family.

It was as if two magnets were pulling on me in opposite directions.

Oh dear God, please help me face the world. I have five beautiful children depending on me. How would Dan handle it if I slipped away? I must be there for them.

Out of my sanctuary, I opened my bedroom door to face reality.

My mind was fractured. I clung to my faith that Jesus loved me and had compassion toward me. Though I didn't understand what was going on, I trusted that He would get me through this darkness and head-spinning confusion.

I had a terrible time keeping my mind focused well enough to take the most rudimentary care of my family. Wrought with mounting depression, it was all I could do to shower and put myself together for the day. Dan did the grocery shopping and dinner prep. I cried, wrote, and read books written by others who had experienced similar losses. I needed to find comfort from somewhere.

When Thanksgiving break was over, I felt that, with God's help, I could hoist myself back into my saddle. However, Miguel had given me time off through Christmas vacation. It relieved me to have more time to process my grief, build some inner strength, and retrieve some focus.

A few weeks went by. I picked up and moved forward, but the pain in my chest never let up. It weighed me down as I pushed my way through each day.

My consolation for Rebecca's stern words was Miguel's sensitivity to how I was feeling over the loss. He seemed to know that my extreme grief was because I was responsible for it. However, even with Miguel's understanding, a feeling like I was being watched wafted through me every time I walked out of my front door.

Dan was my comfort. He let me cry on his shoulder, but he didn't appear to be nearly as affected as I was. My honey was a pillar of strength. His fortitude kept our family grounded and functioning through my turmoil, but I still felt lost and alone.

A few of my closest friends seemed to grasp how I felt. They expressed empathy and held me in their prayers. Without the tender support the Lord provided through them, I can't fathom the depths I would have fallen into.

I kept floating into strange states where I felt like I was passing in and out of dreams. Some were like nightmares, while others were as if I was wrapped in an angel's wings.

I wanted to go home to my mother. She would give me a place where I could get some time to be quiet, pray, and rest my broken spirit. However, in my circumstances, that wasn't a possibility.

With the winter retreat approaching, I clung to the hope that God would move to comfort and restore me. While I packed up our family for another Harding Crest, my spirit implored the Lord's help. I desperately needed His touch.

As we wound our way up the mountain, I stared out my window, watching the scenery blur by. I prayed and wept, anticipating what would happen when we were up there.

I believed the Lord heard my cry and would answer my need. I felt Him surrounding me. I sensed something profound was about to take place.

CHAPTER 34

The Response

We woke up early the first morning of the retreat, dressed, fed the kids, straightened our rooms, and were out the door by eight. After we left the children with their guardians, Dan and I followed the path to the main lodge.

The fire warmed the room. People trickled in, meandered around, and found a chair. Fasting began the night before at midnight, so instead of cups of coffee, many of the people held onto cups of hot water. All the women wore winter hats or their usual lace head coverings. Everyone brought their Bible, and each couple had a hymnal. People had quiet conversations while waiting for Miguel to come and call the meeting to order.

He came in wearing his jeans and a white turtleneck. As usual, his silvery black hair was parted on the side and sprayed slick. He had a businesslike demeanor, typical of his approach to meetings. His wife, Sandi, took a seat in the front row as he spoke with some elders.

When everyone was seated, he stood to face the congregation. One elder opened in prayer. Amos started playing the old upright piano. His masterful fingers always seemed to dance on the keys while we sang our familiar songs. It was our cue to break out praying in tongues when he took his hands off the keys.

Bible in hand, Miguel walked back and forth in front of the podium, seemingly in deep thought. He stopped, turned to face all of us, and then read different verses about speaking truth. "God is spirit, and those who worship Him must worship in spirit and truth." (John 4:24 [NKJV]) "These are the things you shall do: Speak each man the truth to his neighbor. Give judgment in your gates for truth, justice and peace." (Zechariah 8:16 [NKJV])

He motioned to Eleanor. She stood with her white lace veil draped over her brown curly hair. I froze as she turned and looked directly at me.

It was as if I was hit by a lightning bolt. My heart hit bottom like it was dropped from a second- story window. The look on her face told me that this would not be pretty.

"Flori, I'm angry with you."

Oh god.

"I find it ridiculous that because of you, we had to shut down the kindergarten."

Oh dear God, help me. I felt blood rush through my head and threaten to burst from the capillaries in my face.

"You told me you love my son, but I think that nothing could be further from the truth. His heart is breaking because he hasn't been able to have school in a class with the other children. If you truly cared about the kids, you would be there for them."

These words came from a woman who was one of Miguel's right -hand ladies. She was someone I liked and respected. Her tone was a stab in the gut. She sat.

Miguel walked back and forth up front with two fingers pressed against his lips. With his arms still folded, he pointed to another woman. She stood and faced me.

"I'm also upset with you." Her face looked like I disgusted her.

"I think you are making a much bigger deal out of your miscarriage than it is. Women go through them all the time, and they don't fall apart." She sat.

It stunned and hurt to the core. I looked at Dan. He sat stoic, staring straight ahead.

Miguel pointed to Mary-Anne.

Oh no!

Fear squeezed me. She spoke with an angry tone. "You should have returned to school before Thanksgiving break. You have made a much bigger deal out of your miscarriage than is warranted."

I could feel my pulse surging. My face was hot, and my legs shook.

"My sister had a miscarriage the same day you did, and she went back to work the next day." With a smug countenance, she added, "Also, I have to say that I don't like working with you. I feel you are always on edge. It seems as if I am walking on eggshells whenever you're in the classroom with me." Looking as if she was self-satisfied, she sat.

Again, Miguel pointed to another woman, who rose to tell me "You just don't like having to teach, so you're using your miscarriage to get out of it, making the rest of us have to work harder." Her expression seemed to ooze with disdain.

A few other women got up to speak. The things they said insinuated I was a fake and malingerer. It was head-to-toe horror.

When the confrontations and rebukes finally dwindled, Miguel stood in front of the group and said, "Flori, I want you to be thinking of your rebuttal. I want you to tell everyone what you have to say the next time we meet."

A walking wound, I held on to Dan for balance as he led me to our cabin. Dan gathered our kids and fed them lunch. All I could do was lay in a fetal position and sob. Was this the answer to my prayers? I couldn't understand what was happening. My mind was buzzing with static. My heart felt ripped out, kicked up on one side, and stabbed on the other because it didn't beat according to their rhythm.

I'm supposed to come up with a rebuttal. As I cried into my pillow, I tried to think of what to say. Standing before such hostile people, hoping for understanding, seemed futile. I was having trouble holding on to my sanity before. Now this?

The evening meeting came. Miguel had me stand up to explain to the fellowship what I had to say for myself. I spoke but have no recollection of what I tried to say. All I can remember is Frank, an elder and Mary-Anne's husband, stood and said, "What you are saying is nothing but a bunch of crap."

They had flattened me on a gravel road by running me over with a truck. Then they put it in reverse and ran over me again. Just to make sure I was dead.

Then came the following morning meeting. After the usual time of worship and prayer, Miguel stood and spoke. His words are dust in my head. He called on me again. I was not expecting him to ask me to say anything, so my head swirled. I remember standing, but I'm lost as to what I said. I was still in shock, and I didn't know what he expected me to say. Hopelessness and humiliation permeated me as I felt my words falling on deaf ears.

After I sat, Miguel opened his Bible and read a passage that talked about taking care of the weaker member.

Miguel addressed the group.

"As you can see, Flori is not in touch with reality. She is your sister in the Lord, so as members of the body of Christ, it's your responsibility to speak the truth to her when she's out of line. She is what's called a borderline schizophrenic."

Borderline schizophrenic? What's that? Is that the name for what's wrong with me?

He talked about how in the Body of Christ, we are to love and embrace those who are weak. He had me go up front. Then he had everyone stand and form a single line around the room.

I stood next to the podium. Miguel told the group to approach me one at a time and tell me they loved me. Humiliated, I saw everyone standing to wait their turn to speak to me.

Shame covered me like a cold, wet cloak. Confusion spun my thoughts into a blur. I felt like the ball in a pinball machine, flipped from one hug to the next. Each person told me they loved me and hugged me. I had no confidence in how they honestly felt as they embraced me. They just did what they were told.

That afternoon, I was lying on my cot for some rest, when there was a knock on our cabin door. Emily, the current principal of the school, came in and pulled up a chair next to me. *Why is she here?* I sat up.

Softly, she said, "I came to let you know that Miguel has relieved you of your teaching duties."

"What? Why? Am I being disciplined? Why would he relieve me?"

"I don't know. He didn't tell me why. You'll have to ask him."

She didn't seem to be the least bit angry with me. She hadn't stood to confront me for letting the school down.

I sobbed all the way home from the retreat. Not knowing what to think, I felt ripped apart. In the past, they had removed teachers they dealt with for being rebellious or too lenient with the children. I didn't know if I was one of them.

I was too apprehensive to ask Miguel. Fear of being told it was because of my attitude held me captive. Even if it was to pull me out to get rest, the humiliation of being set apart as mentally ill would remain, and the women's anger with me was fire branded on the walls of my heart.

CHAPTER 35

Reeling

We wound our way down the mountain, with our kids bantering and giggling in the back seats. Dan and I were silent, even after all the babes fell asleep. I looked out the window and watched the world go by. Confusion wove strands of dread in my spirit. Tears were hot on my cheeks as I tried to interpret the previous three days.

Father, what are You saying to me? Images of each woman standing to face me stung as they flashed in my head. They seemed hateful. They were the ladies I fellowshipped with and worked around every day. *What do they think of me now that Miguel said I'm a borderline schizophrenic? What's that? Is it the name for how messed up I am? How do I live now? They are supposed to "speak the truth" to me. O my Lord, what does that mean?*

There were no answers.

As we approached the valley, closer to home, a different set of thoughts joined the not -so-merry-go-round in my mind. Things that were going on in the grown-up world had nothing to do with what I wanted for my children—a joyous Christmas. There was a pressing list of things to do in the back of my mind. The calendar didn't stop because I felt like hiding in an obscure hole. I had one day left to prepare.

With my heart in an imaginary burlap sack dragging behind me, I tried to focus on our bubbling brood on Christmas morning. The scroll of things left to do rolled out in front of me.

It was already dark when we arrived home. After we unloaded, fed the kids some sandwiches, and started the laundry, Dan announced that our decorated tree was bone dry. It wasn't safe to turn on its lights. We wanted our tree lit, so we had to find another one. Too exhausted to hit tree lots that night, we had to wait for the following day.

Christmas Eve that year was stress- filled. We couldn't get out to shop for another tree until after sunset. The kids were full of energy, running through the lot, while Dan and I tried to find the least lopsided tree. All I could do was keep moving along and try not to let the pain in my heart pull the whole family down.

After an extensive search, we found one that was decent enough. We went home and spent the rest of Christmas Eve decorating it. When the children were asleep, Dan and I worked to finish wrapping gifts and getting everything set up for the morning.

Weary beyond words, I got through the holiday by clinging to our family traditions and sleeping whenever I could get away with it.

The time came for Tamarisk's annual New Year celebration. They chose our home to host a portion of the progressive dinner. My dear friend Naomi volunteered to help me get ready. I was grateful not to have to get my house set up on my own. Life felt too big to handle by myself. I was carrying an invisible weight through my days and had relentless pain in my chest.

Being able to have Naomi there was comforting. We had known each other since the Blessed Spirit days. She was with me when Elizabeth was born. We hung tight through this walk we were on.

As Naomi finished sweeping, and I was getting ready to clean the bathroom, she called my name.

"Yeah?" I responded.

"There's something I want to tell you."

"What's that?"

"I agree with what the ladies at the retreat were saying. I don't think you should have made such a big issue out of having your miscarriage."

My throat tightened.

"I was ready to go back to school after Thanksgiving. It was Miguel who said to take off until Christmas break."

"Still, I think you are making a much bigger thing of it than it is."

I felt helpless and misunderstood. How could I respond? It was true. Miguel gave me more than enough time to recover from having a miscarriage. Yes, it still hurt, but I didn't think it would keep me from teaching. I didn't know why Miguel decided to take me out of the classroom.

I couldn't comprehend what was going on in my walk with the Lord. Now it seemed impossible to hold mental focus long enough to function at full speed. When I searched my mind for an explanation, I came up empty. How could I defend myself against this profound misunderstanding?

Tears filled my eyes, but I would not let them spill. I hid my face, I picked up my cleaning supplies, and went into the bathroom. The conversation dropped.

That night, our house filled with people. Everyone came for miso soup before they went to Frank and Mary-Anne's house. Their place was the main attraction because they had sushi.

With no appetite for more food, I sat on the hearth next to the fireplace. Its light and warmth were medicine for my aching spirit. Watching the flames dance was soothing. They stilled my mind. I didn't want to talk, but when I entered a conversation to be polite and hostess-like, it was only a few words. I just tried to smile and be pleasant.

Sandi, Miguel's wife, came and sat next to me. Her demeanor was soft.

However, I did not feel the remotest bit comfortable. "How are you doing?" she asked.

My innards shriveled. *What should I say? What kind of answer does she expect?*

"Um, I'm doing OK, pretty much."

I glanced at her eyes but looked away quickly. I didn't trust her. *What would she think if I told her the whole truth? Would I get another sting? I* rationalized it wasn't a lie because I could get up in the morning, put my makeup on, take care of the kids, and get ready for the evening.

I felt guilty for not being bare-naked honest.

We made small talk about Christmas and our New Year's Day parade around the block. Then she stood and went to talk with someone else.

My tension eased.

When I climbed the side step to our bed, I curled up with my pillows. I was finally in my safe place. The icicle in my chest melted into tears.

Is this You, God, speaking to me? These are Your people. Why, when I read the Psalms, am I like the afflicted person crying out to You, and it seems like the fellowships my enemies. How can they be if they're Your people? Who are You? What are You saying to me?

I reached for my cry cloth, an old linen and lace doily. Soft, absorbent, and dainty—perfect for catching tears.

It hurt something fierce to replay the words that came from Naomi, one of my closest friends. I thought she understood my anguish—why it took more than three days for me to get back on my feet. Her outlook put another big crack in my already broken heart.

Wondering why Miguel removed me from teaching was at the forefront of my mind. I didn't know how to process what he dished out to me.

My honey, trying to help, asked Miguel if I was taken out of school to discipline me.

"I asked Miguel why you're not teaching."

"Well, what did he say?"

"Now he's annoyed with you. He says you're impossible to keep happy."

"What does he mean by that?"

"I'm not sure, but I think it's because he sees that you need a break."

The whole thing left me feeling like I was a spectacle. The experience defined humiliation. *What's everyone thinking about me? What's "the truth" that Miguel says everyone is supposed to tell me?* I was afraid of what could happen next.

I knew something was very wrong with my mind. I believed a good psychiatrist could understand what I needed, but there was no way Miguel would let me go to one of "the world's" psychiatric doctors. We had to look to God to take care of our needs. Seeking the world's wisdom was a big no-no.

I cried to my mom over the phone. She didn't agree that I was at fault for my baby's deaths. She seemed worried about me. If she knew everything that was going on, she would take me in so I could run away. But there was no way I would tell her. We had to keep our issues with the church within the covenant.

During the night, I would lie on my bed, look out the window, and pray. *Dear Lord, I don't understand. I'm blind. I cannot see what You are doing. Forgive me for wanting to leave. Help me embrace Your will. I want to learn to bloom where You have planted me. Where is peace?*

Deep down, I thanked God for the time off from teaching. I felt guilty and ashamed, but it was nice to have my activities where I could manage them with reasonable comfort. The only homework I had to be concerned about was my kids. I just had to babysit so I could concentrate on things at home.

CHAPTER 36

Count it All Joy

One cold, rainy night, Dan and I were hanging out by the fire with the kids sprawled out on the floor with their pillows. We were watching television when the phone rang. Dan picked it up and walked to the kitchen.

"Hello?" He muttered some things I couldn't quite hear and then said, "Goodbye."

He came back to the family room. "Frank called. He and Mary-Anne want to come over to talk with you about how you are doing. I told them seven thirty so the kids can be in bed."

Oh no! What's this going to be? My stomach sank, and my heart started pounding. *Try not to panic. Maybe they've mellowed out and aren't upset with me anymore.*

I went to work rousing the children so that I could settle them into their beds. When that was finished, I headed back downstairs to wait for our guests.

There was a knock on the door. Dread hit me in the chest. Dan let the couple in. I greeted them. They took off their coats and sat on the couch in the family room. I sat in front of the fire, facing them. Dan took a seat in his chair next to the window.

For some reason, the details of the conversation elude me, but it wasn't long before I realized that they were there to admonish me to open myself up to the Lord's will for my life. They spoke to me saying things that led me to believe that they were there to point out to me that the reason why I was struggling was that I was stiffening my neck to the leading of the Lord.

Dan sat quietly in his chair. He spoke up and said a few things about how my circumstances had been too much for me to handle, with school and my pregnancies. His words helped me feel supported, but other than that, they fell to the ground.

I was hurt and disappointed. I was left with the impression that Frank and Mary- Anne couldn't see that I had broken down because of the stress and events I had been through. It seemed they saw my condition as a result of the sin in my life. I didn't say much. It was humiliating to find myself feeling defensive.

After they presented their "truth," they gathered their coats, and then we said good night, and they left.

I looked out my bedroom window at the silhouettes of the tops of the trees. I could hear the rush of rain hitting the roof and feel the tears bubble up from my heart and then run over my face.

My Bible was sitting on my bedside table. Feeling the need to find some comfort, I turned to the book of Psalms. As I was reading, I came upon a scripture that seemed to describe how I was feeling. "Hear my prayer, O Lord, and let my cry come to you. Do not hide your face from me in the day of my trouble; incline Your ear to me; in the day that I call, answer me speedily" (Psalm 102:1–2 [NKJV]). I read on and came to "I lie awake, and am like a sparrow alone on the housetop. My enemies reproach me all day long; those who deride me swear an oath against me. For I have eaten ashes like bread, and mingled my drink with weeping, because of Your indignation and Your wrath; for you have lifted me up and cast me away. My days are like a shadow that lengthens, and I wither away like grass" (Psalms 102:7–11 [NKJV]).

Why do I feel like these people are the enemy? How can it be since they are my brothers and sisters in Jesus? I closed my Bible, laid my head on my pillow, and pulled the covers over me.

Is it true that I'm unwilling to face that this is the life that He wants me to embrace? Is it my inability to cope because I don't genuinely desire to follow Him? How can I change my heart and let go of feeling overwhelmed by everything that has gone on? I guess I'll have to pray for the strength to be who He wants me to be.

A piece of my heart gave up hope for any change to come.

A few nights later, the elders came over with a little bottle of oil. Miguel wasn't with them. I welcomed them because I was painfully aware of my need for healing.

I lay on the couch while the deliverance minister rubbed some oil on my forehead. The elders took turns praying for me. I started with eagerness for a special touch from the Lord but ended up with discouragement. While they prayed for me, they rebuked the sin that was keeping me down. It was apparent that they saw my weakened state as a result of my reluctance to go the way the Lord was leading me.

There was no peace or warmth in my heart when they left. I felt hopeless.

The next Sunday in church, Miguel announced that the entire fellowship would be going on a twenty-four-hour fast for me. He talked about the passage in Mark when the disciples couldn't get a demon to come out of someone's child. Jesus said, "This kind can come out by nothing but prayer and fasting" (Mark 9:29 [NKJV]).

I was embarrassed. Sorry that the entire fellowship had to go through something difficult because of me, I wanted to hide. My mental state was causing them to have to sacrifice for me again.

On the appointed day, we all fasted. That night, Dan and I met with elders who were being trained in the deliverance ministry. The whole thing is a weird blur in my memory. I don't recall what was said. I can only remember that I was in a strange state where I felt controlled by a bizarre force while I looked around the room, with my body jerking and twisting. They kept calling the names of various demons, the spirit of this and of that, to come out of me. They told me to cough the demons out. Dan sat in a chair and observed, not having anything to say.

We continued for a few hours until they said that we were finished. They said a closing prayer for the blood of Jesus to cleanse and protect me from the demons' return.

On our way home, I had difficulty figuring out what was real or not real. I floated from one perspective to another. Each state made me feel as though I was more than one person.

The next day, I felt the sort of weird I had grown accustomed to, so I knew it would pass. As I ran across different people in the fellowship, I was asked how I was doing. I mostly said I was OK because the truth was too hard to explain. I thanked them for their prayers.

"My brethren, Count it all joy when you enter into various trials, knowing the testing of your faith produces patience. But let patience have *its* perfect work, that you may be perfect and complete lacking nothing" (James 1:2–4 [NKJV]). "And not only that, but we also glory in tribulations, knowing that tribulation produces perseverance, and perseverance, character; and character, hope (Romans 5:3–4 [NKJV]).

These scriptures mingled with my thoughts and emotions. It was a stretch for me to "count it all joy" and receive what was happening as something to be grateful to God for. I knew I was supposed to embrace what was going on in my life as if it was something for my ultimate good. I wasn't clear on what God was saying to me through all this.

"If any of you lacks wisdom, let him ask of God, who gives to all liberally and without reproach, and it will be given to him" (James 1:5 [NKJV]).

I continued to groan and grapple through my prayers, trying to understand what the Lord wanted to transpire within my heart. All I could see through the circumstances was that His desire was for me to stand through the pain and let go of feeling sorry for myself. He wanted me more durable, so I could bear up to the burden of my responsibilities without complaint. *I am supposed to deny myself, pick up my cross, and follow Him.*

I knew why I felt that something was wrong with the direction they were leading me. How could I change my heart so I could accept the life the Lord had placed me in? My interpretation was I was supposed to give my heart to Him so He could change my feelings to coincide with what they thought was His will. I had to let go of the way my heart wanted to go.

I wanted to be a capable person who took pleasure in doing God's will. The time off I had was for me to get my head straight enough to function the way I was supposed to without breaking down mentally.

My only hope was in the Lord. "Why do you say, O Jacob, and speak O Israel: 'My way is hidden from the Lord, and my claim is passed over by my God'? Have you not known? Have you not heard? The everlasting God, the Lord, the Creator of the ends of the earth neither faints nor is weary. His understanding is unsearchable. He gives power to the weak, and to those who have no might, He increases strength. Even the youths shall faint and be weary, and the young men shall utterly fall, but those who wait on the Lord shall renew their strength; they shall mount up with wings like eagles, they shall run and not be weary, they shall walk and not faint" (Isaiah 40:27–31 [NKJV]).

So I waited.

CHAPTER 37

Absolved

The wind blew the dark clouds of winter apart. Tiny white blossoms graced the tree in our front yard. The promise of warm days ahead lifted my spirit. A new inner strength developed in me. My ability to stay focused returned, and I felt capable of managing my family and church responsibilities.

One day Sandi called me and asked how I was doing. I told her I was doing well. She asked if I felt ready to take on the job of substitute coordinator for the teachers in the school.

Wow, a position that has authority! I was honored; they thought I could oversee something. They put me back in good standing. The sub-coordinator made sure all the bases got covered when a teacher couldn't make it to school. It was something that would keep me on the phone a lot, but it was a job I could do at home. I accepted, as if I had a choice. So for the rest of the school year, I saw to it the school had the teachers it needed to keep running. I enjoyed the challenge of managing flu season.

Another trip to Bodega Bay and our family vacation in Tahoe came to pass. They called me back into the kindergarten as a reading and math teacher for the coming school year. Planning for it was much easier than before because I was familiar with what I needed to do. Since it was Luke's kindergarten year, he would be in the classroom with me, but Ms. Annie taught his group.

Annie was a wonderful lady to work with. She was one of the tenderhearted women who was empathetic and supportive when I lost my babies. We were a good team, pouring our hearts into instructing the children. The humor and camaraderie between us energized and lifted my spirit. When times for tears came, we gave each other a place to get love and comfort.

Soon after school started, I found that I was pregnant again. A wall went up between my head and my heart that kept my hopes at bay. I didn't get morning sickness, and early on, I started spotting. I went to see Marilee. She determined there was no heartbeat.

Early the next morning, while the anesthesiologist was getting ready to put a mask over my face, Marilee whispered a prayer into my ear. I wanted to go to sleep and never wake up.

The next thing I knew, I reentered life after a miscarriage. It hurt and discouraged me, but a rigidity had formed in my core. I was determined not to break. It was a Friday, so I had two full days to get a foothold before having to put my hands to the plow and forge forward.

Before the kids came into the classroom, Miguel came in as I was putting the finishing touches on the Thanksgiving bulletin board. He told me that because I miscarried early on, no baby had formed, so it was a "blighted ovum." He assured me it was not my fault; I didn't kill a baby.

I took him at his word, believing that he knew what he was talking about. What he said went down like warm pudding on a snowy day. The feeling of relief was so great—I didn't hurt after that. The loss became a mere fact of life, nothing to get upset about. I was absolved.

CHAPTER 38

More Paint for the Picture

Couples sat scattered on the cushioned pews in the sanctuary. Golden light came through the stained glass windows resting on the lace veils the women wore. The young children were being cared for by the teenagers back in the classrooms.

I wasn't there because I wanted to be, but I tried to make the best of it.

Better that than descend into some murky mood.

Miguel was doing his customary pacing before he stopped and looked up at us. "Family, it's time we come to a consensus regarding what we will to do about using birth control. It's not good that we are doing different things."

Everyone who wanted to stood and voiced their point of view. Miguel interjected scriptures about the Body of Christ having one mind. "Now the multitude of those who believed were of one heart and one soul" (Acts 4:32 [NKJV]). "Now may the God of patience and comfort grant you to be like- minded toward one another, according to Christ Jesus, that you may be with one mind and one mouth glorify the God and Father of our Lord Jesus Christ" (Romans 15:5–6 [NKJV]).

The fellowship bantered back and forth about whether to leave the size of our families up to God to decide. Since Dan and I gave up using birth control much earlier, I didn't find the idea threatening. However, not all the women wanted to be a baby factory, and many families were struggling to make ends meet. At the conclusion of our discussion, Miguel mandated us not to use contraception.

Bellies with bumps of various sizes were part of the texture and atmosphere within the covenant. Babes under blankets lay across their mothers' laps. Diaper bags hung on shoulders throughout our daily activities. Our quivers grew.

During one of our drawn-out covenant meetings, Miguel paced in front of the sanctuary. He spoke for a while and then paused. "Family, there's an issue that needs to be addressed. Some of you mothers are nursing your infants on demand. You should feed your newborns every four hours."

Frank stood and read a passage from a book he had been reading. It was about how babies are born self- absorbed and demanding of our attention. Miguel said that it was our responsibility to discipline our infants so they don't develop into selfish beings. They need to learn that they do not come first in this world.

By feeding them on demand, we were reinforcing selfish behavior. We should make them fit into our schedule, not the other way around.

The subject was not up for discussion. It was an instruction Miguel expected us to follow. For me, it was like running into a wall.

Four hours? Unbelievable! My babies always nursed on demand, which was every two to three hours. I balked at the thought of making a newborn wait so long between feedings.

I felt violated. The time I spent with my babies was sacred to me. It was as if Miguel had penetrated a core dominion—a part of my life that belonged to me to govern as I saw fit.

A flame ignited inside me. It was the same burning anger I thought was killing my unborn children. Fortunately, I didn't have an infant, so I could put off worrying about it. The feeling dissipated.

As teachers in the school, it was our job to teach the children obedience. Being mothers who loved our children, we did our best to do it positively. We did a lot of praising for the children's efforts to learn and follow instructions.

There was a darker side—Miguel's consequences. He grew to be extremely harsh. The rules the children had to follow at school were ridged.

He grew meticulous and moody. Everything had to be just so. He was a neat freak and expected perfect obedience in maintaining his standards. The children had to line their shoes up, heels first, against the outer wall of the classrooms. There was a myriad of other nitpicky stuff. He ran a tight ship, insisting the adults be addressed with a "Yes, sir" and "Yes, ma'am" after being given a direct command, etc. When children failed to follow instructions or seemed to be the least bit defiant, Miguel instructed us to send them to him for a "correction." At first, it was a hard swat on the buttocks with a wooden paddle. After a while, he started using a PVC pipe on their hands.

Every time they received a swat, a check was put on their homework tag. When they got home, their father was supposed to administer the same number of swats as there were checkmarks.

I worked mainly in kindergarten. I don't recall ever finding it necessary to send anyone to the office. That sort of thing happened mostly with the older kids.

CHAPTER 39

Bloom Where We're Planted

Raising a child "in the way he should go" was much more than just the way we were to correct our kids. As mothers and teachers, we focused on God being the center of everything. We kneaded loving the Lord and one another into everything we taught. We tried to impart faith, hope, charity, diligence, humility, and kindness as we went through our lessons. Our vision was to do good and be pleasing to the Lord.

We poured our hearts into educating the children. Watching over them like mother hens, we paid attention to where the children were in their understanding of the concepts being covered and adjusted to fit their needs. Each child was unique.

Learning was a lot of hard work on the kids' parts, but we tried to make it as interesting and fun as we could. Once per month, field trips were a requirement. Every month we put up new bulletin boards that were like works of art. The school was a bustling place of learning and camaraderie.

The women worked on running the school through all maternal conditions. They gave us time off just before we were due to have a baby. The moms who had an infant usually babysat so they could stay home with the newest member of their family. During my time off from teaching, I babysat.

I take my hat off to the women who worked to keep up with childcare. Most women were part of the organized flurry, although it didn't seem as if Sandi was as much a part of the operation anymore. Maybe it's because I didn't witness it. She lived within eyeshot of the knoll in my front yard, directly in the center of all the neighborhood activities.

Carpooling was a big part of the whole effort. The people who lived beyond walking distance from Candlewick dropped their kids off to ride the rest of the way to school. Our twelve-passenger van was part of the caravan. We drove one another's cars regularly to make things go smoothly.

Through our activities, we became close. We knew one another well. Some got along very well, while others frequently rubbed edges. Confessions and confrontations were a way of life. We wouldn't have been able to function as well as we did if we held unforgiveness toward one another and didn't have God's love at work in our lives.

It cultivated dear friendships as we suffered through our trials and tribulations. We leaned on one another and held one another up in prayer. We rejoiced and wept together.

I got over the hurt from the season of accusation I went through after I lost my babies. I didn't continue to hold it against the women who confronted me. They knew not what they did. It was because of the pressure to run the school. If a teacher was out, the burden fell on others.

Naomi remained my good friend. There was a particular bond between us that repaired the wound from the day we were cleaning together. She became an island I could swim to for some R & R. She amazed me with how like the Proverbs 31 woman she was. She was industrious beyond what the church demanded of her and still seemed calm.

We planned a getaway to Lake Tahoe. We'd stay at my mom's and spend our time reading magazines while baking our bodies in the warm summer sun on the beach. It turned out to be imprinted in my mind.

The temperature was perfect, right on the cusp between warm and hot. There was a light breeze. Geese came and ate chips we tossed at them. We lay on our tummies, thumbing through magazines, and then turned sunny-side up to brown our fronts.

We got up, walked down the beach, and talked. Our table of contents covered a wide range of subjects. Our conversation took us to the end of the beach property and back to our towels. All the details escape me, but I know the basic gist of it.

I can almost hear Naomi's voice as I recall her expressing how frustrated she was about having to be in the Tamarisk Covenant Fellowship. She wanted to run away to San Luis Obispo. She didn't intend to because it would split her family. Naomi was angry with her husband for getting them involved.

Me? I wanted to move out into the country and live a simple, wholesome life with my husband and children. I thought it would be good for the children to grow up where it was harder to get involved with "the world." I still had my admiration for the Amish.

Both of us wanted to be able to live like other Christians and be free to make our own choices. Having to go up to the Harding Crest retreat just before Christmas and being too busy were our mutual dislikes. We talked about how crazy it was to have to pack the diaper bags and lunches a certain way, or you'd get penalized. There were people who would turn us in.

We came back to our little day camp site and continued to talk.

"Look at the school. The children are getting a good education," I said.

"We couldn't have it unless we were all laying down our lives."

As we were packing up to go back to my mom's house, I stopped what I was doing. "Naomi?"

"Yeah?"

"For some crazy reason, God has put our seeds in this ground. It's our choice to either be miserable or bloom where we're planted."

CHAPTER 40

You're Leaving Again?

Dan frequently had to go out of town for business. This left me to handle the entire household without his support. It overwhelmed me. With so much we needed to stay on task for, I became a very tense mommy. I complained every time Dan was preparing to leave and when he returned home.

Miguel caught wind of my problem. He had a solution. He put Jerry, the elder across the street, in charge of disciplining our kids when they weren't compliant while Dan was away. I was to call Jerry every time one of the children needed "a correction."

One evening, Matthew was giving me a hard time for some long-forgotten reason. I called Jerry for some backup. He told me to send Matthew over to his house.

When he came home, I could tell from how he walked that Jerry must have been exceptionally hard on him. I asked Matthew if he would show me his backside. What I saw remains branded on my heart. Jerry struck my poor son so he bruised to the point his skin had tiny beads of blood on it.

It made me sick to my stomach. However, all I did was sympathize with how much he was hurting. I warned him and the rest of our children about how terrible it would be to have to go over to Jerry's. I admonished them to be obedient and put them to bed.

If I told Jerry what I was feeling and thinking, I would come against an elder. That could mean trouble from leadership and probably not change anything.

There was a knock at the door. It was Jerry. He asked me what I thought about what happened with Matthew.

I felt like I was walking on tenuous ground. I loathed what Jerry had done and didn't think it was right for him to do it. Fear of confronting him placed a guard on my tongue. It's as if I shrank into a wimp. I told him I didn't like it and thought it was unnecessary to hit that hard.

Jerry's countenance was upbeat. It seemed to me he asked out of pure curiosity. He made a joke about me being "ovarian."

The next day, Dan came home with a brace on his leg. He was struggling with the pain and other issues of a torn ligament in his knee. Somehow what happened to Matthew got lost in the pile of luggage and flurry of activity surrounding Dan's homecoming and injury.

CHAPTER 41

Bible Study

Miguel held a Bible study for the youth eleven years old up through the high school age. When Matthew was old enough to join, we were told there was total confidentiality about what went on during the meetings.

I bristled. In my mind, that was a red flag. I felt that as parents, we had a right to know what was happening in the group. Dan agreed with me. When we brought the issue up to Miguel, he told us it was imperative that the youth did not share any details because it would hinder the kids from being open to sharing their innermost thoughts and feelings. He said it was to prevent gossip about their sensitive issues.

This made some sense to me, though I still had a hesitant gut feeling about it. However, there was no arguing with Miguel. It was another way we laid our feelings down and went along.

Being a part of the study was a rite of passage. It distinguished the bigger from the little kids. It was a badge of honor that required a lot of work but had perks to look forward to, such as going to Magic Mountain for the weekend, ski trips, and opportunities to go to the movies.

During the years Matthew and Mark were part of the study, Dan and I heard little about the things Miguel orchestrated with the group since the kids couldn't talk about what went on. We knew that Miguel was strict and required intense memorization of scripture, but we had little to go on when it came to the details of issues that arose during their times together. All we knew about it was that our boys spent a lot of time with their Bibles. I was proud of them for working so diligently.

We heard that Miguel was very demanding in his expectations. He was hard to please and punitive with anyone who missed his mark. The consequences were extreme.

When Mark was the youngest member of the group, he was at a disadvantage. The older kids were far more accustomed to where the various books of the Bible were and well-practiced at locating scriptures quickly. When Miguel called them to find a verse. They would race to see who could get there the fastest. Mark was always last to find it. It was a rule that the last person who reached it had to run a lap around the schoolyard in their socks. Mark was almost always the underdog.

Being a member of the study was a privilege easy to lose. The kids were required to memorize long passages of the Bible. Then they had to repeat them in front of the group.

One such time, Matthew memorized an entire chapter. He could recite it perfectly at home. The day came for him to say it in front of the Bible study. He stumbled on one word, corrected himself, and then finished the chapter. It was not good enough for Miguel, but he offered him the chance to try again the next day.

Before the group met, some kids were in the corridor looking at something. Curious, Matthew went to see what. It was a book one of the girls had been assigned to check out of the public library. It contained something written about the zodiac signs. Miguel found out. He labeled them all as getting involved with witchcraft. Because Matthew was one of them, he couldn't recite his chapter. Therefore, he was not allowed back into the Bible study.

Shunning was a tool Miguel used to coerce members of the fellowship. The children were no exception. One time, Matthew was down the street playing football with his friends. I called him to come home for dinner. He told the others it was time for him to leave and asked them to give him his football. The other kids wanted to use it. Matthew said no. Miguel labeled Matthew as selfish. He told all the children they were to avoid him and not speak to him at all.

After this, a boy in the study had to stay with us because his parents were out of town. While at home, Matthew asked him a question, which he answered. Somehow it came to Miguel's attention. He ordered them to soak paper towels with liquid soap and stuff them in their mouths. They had to face the Bible study group. Then he had the boys pull their pants down to their underwear in front of them. He swatted them ten times with a PVC pipe. After that, he made them hold the towels in their mouths for ten more minutes.

There are many other horror stories told about things that happened with people's kids during the Bible study years that we were not aware of because of Miguel's confidentiality rule.

We were not told how into sexual sin Miguel was. He looked for it in the kids. They had to confess. If they did not ever confess something, he would accuse them of lying. He broke up close friendships between two people, forbidding them to hang out together. They could only have minimal contact.

There were numerous other testimonies exposed by the participants, but they are not my stories to share.

CHAPTER 42

A Prayer

One night while washing the dishes, I watched out the window as the brilliant colors of sunset painted the sky beyond silhouettes of the Italian cypress trees lining our back fence. The day had been sunny and warm, but the climate in my heart was gray and damp. I longed for the joy that we sang about in church but seemed to be unattainable for me.

Frustrated, I thought I needed to accept my life as it was. I wanted to please God, but my desire for more freedom just would not die. A pleading prayer birthed from the innermost part of me. I could feel my spirit take flight to carry it to the one who made the magnificent scene before me. Though I was silent, I could almost hear my cry resounding in the heavenlies.

"Oh, Father, why do we have to live like this? I want things to be different for our family. I'm always uptight, and the kids have constant pressure to perform. Is it honestly supposed to be like this? Isn't there another way to serve You? Do we have to stick so tight to this fellowship?"

I knew God heard my prayer, but in His silence, I sank into resignation.

⚮

Driving the van full of kids and groceries into our neighborhood, I spotted Roxy, one of the elder's wives, through the open door of their garage. She was fingering a head- shaped mound of clay. Roxy was a breath of fresh air. She had a tender, grandmotherly spirit, bubbling with creativity.

I parked in our driveway, put Elizabeth on my hip, and left the older kids to bring the bags into the house. I headed over to Roxy. She was working on a clay bust of her daughter. We chatted about her project and the ballet classes she was giving to the young girls of our fellowship. Her easy smile and cheerful eyes melted my guard and loosened my tongue.

"I love how you are able to work on all kinds of art. You seem to always come up with something new." Switching my toddler to the other hip, I added, "There are things I would enjoy doing if I could get around to it."

"Like what?"

"I would plant flowers all over my front yard. Look how cheerful your home looks with all your roses and irises. There just isn't enough of me."

"I used to feel the same way. I had more ideas than time. Things are different now that my children have grown and left home."

Fascinated, I watched her skillful fingers smooth the nose and cheekbones of her bust.

"It seems like I'll never be able to."

"Oh, honey," she soothed, "your children are still young and tucked under your feathers. They still need all you can give. It won't be forever though." She dipped her hands in a bucket of water. Wiping them off, she said, "I've learned over the years that life will always bring changes."

"Mom, watch!" I heard the children calling and looked to see them doing somersaults down the hill of our lawn.

"I better get going. It's almost dinnertime."

Roxy touched me on the shoulder.

"Just remember, nothing ever stays the same."

Miguel and Larry stood straight- faced at the pulpit. Miguel opened by telling the congregation a brief history of the journey they'd had over the years. The details drifted into my ears, where they got lost in whatever else I had on my mind.

When Larry moved in front of the microphone, dread stilled my stomach. His messages had a way of leaving me feeling like I was falling short of what God wanted from me. It was as if he was more attuned to God and a much stronger Christian than me. He always seemed to have a stern, gray countenance. I cringed every time he told me that he loved me. I couldn't understand how he could say that, even though he barely knew me.

He talked about the health problems that were plaguing him. His asthma was so bad he always struggled to breathe. Because continued prayer seemed to be unfruitful, he believed God was leading him to follow his doctor's advice and move to a different climate. He told us that he and Roxy were leaving us to live in Arizona.

I could have jumped and danced. *If God can lead one of Miguel's main men to leave, then it's possible for Him to open doors to other places far away from here. Hallelujah! There's hope.*

CHAPTER 43

Sonogram

Because I had three consecutive miscarriages, Marilee ran a series of tests to see if there was an underlying cause. Everything came up clear. She concluded that there was nothing wrong with me that would interfere with another pregnancy.

I was happy, though still anxious about the possibility of going through another loss. I was familiar enough with my body to know when it was time to abstain. Dan was upbeat about being open to it. He said he didn't want us worry. His attitude blessed me and helped ease my mind.

I couldn't help being thrilled when I had a positive test. There was something about having a baby growing inside me. It lifted me and enriched my life. Dan's countenance gave me strength and encouragement. He seemed confident this time would be different.

It wasn't long before I felt the familiar sensations of morning sickness take hold. Even though I felt tired and ill, it heartened me because it was a sign that things were progressing as they should. My hopes soared.

After a few weeks of nausea, it seemed like I was feeling better. *Oh, not again. My baby's dead.*

One morning at school, I became overwhelmed with anxiety. On my first break, I called the doctor. Bless her, she said I could go into her office for a sonogram. Eleanor said she would cover for me, so I left, biting my lip all the way there.

"Praise be to Jesus! My baby's heart is beating!"

Marilee said that it looked like the baby was coming along just fine. Exuberant, I drove back to school, announced my good news, and finished my work.

The school was out for the day. Children were doing their cleanup duties and gathering in the corridor to join their carpools. I spotted Miguel walking from the parking lot toward the school. I rushed to him to announce my happy news.

He responded with a look of impatience and disgust. I stood shocked as he berated me in front of the kids for my lack of faith and spiritual immaturity. His voice pierced me. I cannot recall what he said. All I can remember is standing there, tears pouring, hurt, and humiliated in front of my young audience.

He told me to go into his office, where he sat across from me, watching me cry. After a while, he tenderly handed me some tissues and spoke soothingly. I remember nothing he said except, "Of course, your baby is just fine. You have no reason to worry."

I was confused but relieved. After we talked for a while, I felt warmed and encouraged. I drove home, rejoicing in the Lord that all was well.

Thinking back, I called Dan several times throughout the day. My honey helped me keep my balance. We had a lot to celebrate when he came home.

CHAPTER 44

Brainwashed

School was out for the day. Some kids were busy vacuuming and sweeping; others were scurrying around, getting their things ready to go home. The phone in the hallway rang. It was for me. My dear friend and babysitter Annabelle was on the line.

"Hi?" I questioned. It was strange to get a call right before the carpools headed out unless it was an emergency.

"What's up?"

"I need to tell you something." Her tremulous voice rang an alarm.
"Is everything OK?"

"Elizabeth ignored me when I told her it was time to come in. I told her several times, but she wouldn't obey me."

Oh my god, what's she going to say?

"She wouldn't hold still so I could give her a swat. I didn't know what to do, so I called Miguel."

Uh-oh. "What did Miguel say?"

"He was at home, so he told me to walk her over there." She paused. I gasped.

"He gave her a correction."

I knew, at that point, it was horrible.

"I just want you to know before you come home."

My stomach turned into quicksand. My heart seemed to race at every red light.

Annabelle met me at my front door.

"I think she'll be all right, but she wouldn't hold still."

"Where is she?"

"Upstairs in her room."

Elizabeth was lying down on her tummy. The first thing I saw was her bruised hands. *He must have come down on her while she was trying to protect herself.*

"Oh, my baby girl, what happened?"

She reached for me with tears in her eyes. All I knew to do was rock her gently in my arms. I knew there had to be more gruesome news on her bottom, but I had to brace myself before I could look. I was unprepared to see what came next. It took my breath away.

I checked her out to make sure she wasn't hurt beyond bruises. They were deep, but they would heal on their own. Everything would be OK if no one saw her. It unnerved me to think if someone did, they would turn us into Child Protection Services. We would lose our children.

"Flori, how is she?"

I turned to look at Annabelle.

"She looks horrible. What happened?"

"I told her to come in the house several times. She wouldn't obey me. I went to give her a correction, but she wouldn't hold still. I called Miguel and asked him what I should do. He told me to walk her over to his house. He took us to his garage office and said he would show me how to handle it. She wouldn't hold still for him either."

"But look what he did! This is reprehensible!"

"I know, Flori, I'm so, so sorry. I had no idea he would do this. She kept twisting around and putting her hands in the way."

"She had to be terrified and trying to protect herself. I'm sure God didn't mean this when He said to use the rod."

When Annabelle left, I sat with Elizabeth, petting her head while she lay quietly and stared into the distance. Feelings I didn't know how to cope with spun me into emotional paralysis. I couldn't move as thoughts played crack-the-whip. *What am I going to do? This is unbearable.*

Why Miguel? How could you do this to my baby? There is no way she deserved anything like this. Fears caged my braising anger.

What will I say if someone outside our fellowship sees her? Miguel did this. I will either have to tell on him, which would expose God's delegated authority, or let them believe I did it. If I said Miguel did it, then everyone could lose their children. It would be all my fault. I could tell the bruises would take time to heal. What if she gets sick and needs to see the doctor?

My gaze landed on Elizabeth's bruised hands. *This is unbelievable. I can't let this fly without confronting him for beating my little girl.* Fear snared the mama bear in me. *What's he going to say? I'm sure he thinks this is OK. My feelings will not change his mind. Even so, I can't sit on how upset I am. If I keep this inside of me, it could kill the baby in my womb.* After sitting there for a while to gather my courage, I picked up the phone.

"Hello, this is Miguel."

"It's Flori."

"Yes, I was expecting to hear from you. You think I was too hard on her."

"Yes, I do, and I'm upset. What you did isn't like a correction. It looks like a beating."

"I thought you would say that. Your ovarian. Mothers can't handle this sort of thing."

"What do you mean?"

"It was necessary to teach her to hold still while receiving a swat. The kids aren't supposed to fight their corrections. They are supposed to hold still."

"But she's just a little girl. Of course, she moved around. She was scared."

"The problem isn't with me. It's with Dan. If he were handling discipline properly, she would have known to be still. It's the easiest way to get through it."

"I still think it was beyond necessary."

"Of course, you would. Mothers are always trying to stand in the way of letting God deal with their children."

"What if someone sees her like this?"

"There's no need to worry. Anytime you need to go anywhere, I will see to it that someone in the fellowship watches her."

It was no use in talking to him. He wouldn't take me seriously. I ended the call.

I reached Dan at his office and told him what had happened. He came home as soon as he could. After he saw the condition of our daughter, he said he needed to talk to Miguel and went out the door.

He came back with his shoulders down. He said Miguel told him it was his fault because he wasn't firm enough with the children. I don't know what he was thinking or how he was dealing with this inside himself, but I could tell his heart was heavy.

I was in turmoil. I hated what Miguel did to my sweet little Elizabeth. Again, I thought about the baby inside me. *What are my overwhelming feelings going to do to this child?* I didn't know how to swim through the tsunami of thoughts and emotions, slamming me against the rocks of reality. The thought of someone outside our fellowship seeing her in this condition petrified me.

I couldn't contain myself into total inaction. There were some women in the fellowship I felt would understand my feelings without judging me for being rebellious. I called for some empathy and advice.

I told my friend Nadine what happened. She understood how sick I was feeling. She had walked in my shoes and knew how hard it was to accept how Miguel was with the children. Over the next few days, I ran the situation by some other women. Elizabeth wasn't alone. I heard other stories of similar things happening to their children as well. I wasn't the only mother struggling to accept such a thing as being OK.

Time passed. Elizabeth's bruises faded into a bad memory. It relieved me that no one saw her. Dan and I would have surely lost our children.

My anger toward Miguel dissipated into subliminal unrest. I couldn't believe that what he had done was what God's Word meant when it talked about using a rod to discipline a child. However, I released it to the Lord. *Miguel will have to face God with this.*

CHAPTER 45

Quickening

At the end of the school year, we had a special outing to a nearby lake to go boating. Everyone involved with the school packed picnic lunches and set up a day camp at the beach.

The children had a blast taking turns in the boat. The older ones water-skied or got towed on an inner tube, while the young ones played at the water's edge. It was a celebration for the mothers because most of our school responsibilities were off our shoulders for half of the summer.

My tummy was growing, and my checkups were going well. It was time for me to be less sick and have more energy. Feeling good was something to be happy about.

When our group was sun-kissed and covered in dirty sand, we dragged our gear to our cars. At home, Dan and I pulled our cargo out of the van and spread it out on the lawn. While we were letting the air out of our raft, I sat on the grass to rest.

Then … *What was that?* I felt a slight flutter deep below my belly button. I waited for a few minutes. Nothing more. I bent over to fold the raft. *There, it's more robust this time. Could it be?* I sat back, held still, and breathed slowly, anticipating. *There it is again.* "Honey, I can feel the baby moving!"

If a bird flew across our yard, he would have seen a daddy and mommy hugging in the driveway and a bunch of kids playing with the hose on the front lawn strewn about with beach paraphernalia.

A happy day.

CHAPTER 46

Respite

Dan's family loved camping. While he and his siblings were growing up, they spent their family vacations tenting it up and down the state of California. It was their form of fun and relaxation and has provided them with a multitude of warmhearted memories.

My outlook was that the planning, packing, setting up, and surviving hard sleeping surfaces, distant toilet and shower facilities, along with other inconveniences were not my idea of leisure time. The cleanup that followed such adventures was enough to give me a strong disdain for the whole concept. My father-in-law made light of my sentiments. He gave me a bumper sticker that said, "My Idea of Camping Is When Room Service Is Late."

It had been several years since the Paquette clan had sang around the campfire. Dan's parents organized a trip for everyone to meet at one of their favorite spots in the mountains. Naturally, Dan was enthusiastic about the idea.

I wanted to run away and hide. We had just finished cleaning up from a sopping wet church trip to Bodega Bay. The last thing I wanted to do was drag our kids and my pregnant body up to the woods and then live out of a tent for another week. Dan wouldn't accept my virulent point of view. Fishing with his dad, swimming in a mountain lake, and hiking with the kids won the day. He assured me by telling me the toilets flushed, there were hot showers, and he would see to it I had extra soft padding for my sleeping comfort. It appeased me when he promised coffee in my hands as soon as I got up in the morning.

We pitched our tent at a site near the bathroom. As promised, the toilets flushed. However, to my absolute horror, there were no hot water or showers. There weren't any mirrors. *How will I see to put my makeup on? Even Bodega Bay was better than this.* I was white-hot angry at Dan for not making sure there were proper facilities for bathing the children and electrical outlets so I could blow-dry my hair.

I was alone in my plight. To me, everyone else was having a delightful time, including my husband. It seemed he was saying, "I'm sorry, but it's just the way it's going to be."

There was only one thing left to do. Hence, I crawled onto my sleeping bag, which Dan had made sure was soft and comfortable. I expelled my hot tears and growled into my pillow.

When I woke, I was so comfortable I didn't want to get up. My anger toward Dan was now just feeling sorry for myself. There was no way out of this. So began the journey to acceptance.

Paquette voices from my in- laws' camp danced in my ears. Their spot was like the family room in a house. Uncle Joe's laughter and the scent of dinner on the grill welcomed me to this family event in the woods.

After we cleaned up the dinner dishes, out came the smores. We spread ourselves around the fire, over-ate, and found funny things to talk about. Uncle Joe and Aunt Susan were telling their jokes. Everyone was laughing, including me.

Then Joe came out with his prize- winning joke. I must not repeat it. It was crude and had a punch line that rang the bell. I laughed harder than I had cried. That short story defined hilarious.

I could not help myself. It took work for me to stop snickering. This doesn't say nice things about my character, but at least I could still laugh.

The next morning, my little blessing welcomed me to a new day. It was impossible to stay upset with the wonder in my womb, reminding me all is well. I couldn't stay in bed with my other babies up and into things. I didn't want to have to reorganize the tent. But first, it was time for coffee. I crawled out of my nest and headed for the smiles and good mornings that awaited me. A day of the sweet mountain air, the walkabouts along the trails, and the discovery of a trailer in town with coin-operated shower stalls had amazing effects on my mood. I loved watching our children run free, play in the lake, and hike through the woods. I called Dan honey again.

Day 7 arrived. I had such a good time I didn't want to go home to the hardest part of camping—the cleanup along with tasks of getting ready for school. Only the Lord knew what drama the fellowship would have on the menu.

As we drove home, I felt a tight heaviness replacing the warm lightness of the past week. It was oppressive. But my baby was kicking, and I wanted to keep it that way. Therefore, I had to work on my attitude.

CHAPTER 47

Dr. Yee

The baby's kicks and hiccups meant that things were good for the day. As my due date drew near, I began worrying that we weren't right with God because we never asked our doctor if he would refer a woman to another doctor for an abortion. It was something we were told to do. It was no longer the special of the day on the church's menu. However, it kneaded my thoughts like chewing gum.

I went to Dan about it. Again, he said not to worry. No matter. Guilt fueled the fear that burned my spirit. In my mind, we were disobedient; therefore, God may take our baby from us.

I was anxious about approaching Dr. Yee. *What if he says yes? We'll have to leave him. How can we tell him goodbye?*

Caught between choices was a hard place to be—face our beloved doctor or disobey God.

Dr. Yee took his time before answering my question. I could almost hear the gears turning in his head. Then he spoke. "It doesn't matter how I feel about abortion. I am a doctor. I have a responsibility to see to it my patients have all the proper treatment to keep them healthy."

My heart broke.

Later in the evening, Dan and I talked about what Dr. Yee said. Dan spoke his mind.

"I don't think we should have to leave him. I already said that, and I haven't changed my mind."

"But what about the baby?"

"It will be just fine."

"I'm still afraid."

"Then if it will make you feel better, we can find another doctor."

The whole situation made me heartsick. Deep down, I was angry. It was another time of going against my desire. However, I was too afraid that God would take our unborn child.

The thought of having to look Dr. Yee in his eyes to tell him the unpalatable was too much for me. I took the coward's way out and prayed my letter didn't hurt him.

CHAPTER 48

A Day Remembered

I lay in bed a while longer than usual, feeling my Braxton-Hicks contractions, hoping that this would be labor day. Even though it wasn't my due date, I was more than ready. My little four-year-old Elizabeth climbed into bed with me. She liked opportunities to put her hands on my tummy and feel the baby kicking. It was a fasting day, so I was in no hurry to get out of bed. Nothing but water until dinner. I had no hot cup of coffee to motivate me.

Betsy, Dan's mom, was helping the kids get off to school. She came from the Bay Area to help me out when the baby arrived. The children loved their grandma Betsy, and Grandma Betsy loved them. I think she was the best mother-in-law anyone could ever ask for.

Dan and I were planning to meet with several of the guys we knew from our first church in Chico. We planned to meet at a town an hour and a half away from our home. It was something we were excited about because it was ten years since we'd seen each other. We planned to break our fast when we joined them at the restaurant.

First, I had my one-week checkup with Marilee. After she examined me, she told Dan and me it could be any time. We told her about our plan to leave town to visit with our friends. She gave her familiar sideways look with a pressed smile, shook her head, and said it would be risky. We told her how much it meant to us. She said it was our decision to make.

We were ready for anything. We had our emergency childbirth kit if the time came before we could make it to the hospital. We couldn't miss this long-awaited opportunity.

It was exciting to see the guys' faces again. I was the only woman there. Our group sat on a curved bench seat. We scrunched around the table, greeting one another, and chatting about our lives. Since I was ready to have our sixth baby, Dan and I were a big focus of attention.

The waitress brought our menus. It was past six o'clock in the evening, so Dan and I could break our fast. My eager eyes scanned over the dishes while the men chatted.

When the waitress came to check on us, the dam broke. I gasped. The men looked up and stared at me while my water spread over the seat onto the floor. The looks on our friends' faces were prize-winning. Surprise and shock, laced with delight and wonder of what to do next, bubbled around our table.

They gathered around me and escorted me out to our car. We all laughed, hugged, and said goodbye. Dan raced through the congested traffic back to our city. I was on the phone to tell my friends at home to meet us when we got there.

My closest friends were already at the hospital. We rushed up to the maternity ward, thinking I would have the baby soon. Not so. I strolled the halls with Dan and my ladies-in-waiting for a few hours before my pains rendered me unable to walk.

Before the evening's end, our little John was born. Joy beyond words satiated me. It seemed like the Holy Spirit kissed me on the forehead, a touch from God I will never forget. The Lord heard my prayers and had mercy on me. "You have turned my mourning into dancing; You have put off my sackcloth and clothed me with gladness, to the end, that my glory may sing praise to You and not be silent. O Lord my God, I will give thanks to you forever" (Psalm 30:11–12 [NKJV]).

CHAPTER 49

The Open Door

The fellowship had just settled down in the sanctuary for another covenant meeting. *I wonder how long this one will be. What are we going to talk about this time?* I sighed, rolling my eyes.

Miguel stood up front and announced his latest brainstorm. He said we had come to a crossroads. We couldn't move on to where the Lord was leading without everyone's heart fully committed. "We are heading into places where we must be strong. There can be no weak links in our chain."

Hmm, I wonder what he has in mind now.

"Therefore, the door is open. Anyone who doesn't want to serve the Lord with us can go ahead and leave. You are set free with no recrimination from the Lord."

What? Is he serious? Could this be real?

The room went still. I felt my pulse throb, and my hopes explode from their prison cell. I peeked through my eyelashes to see if I could catch glimpses of the faces in the room. My eyes met Dan's, and we looked at each other, eyebrows raised.

"This is the only time you will have this opportunity. After this, it's until death does us part. So I want you to go home and seriously consider where your heart is. Make up your mind. Are you going to walk with us? Because, if you aren't, it's time for you to leave."

✳

On the way home, I was dancing with glee behind my subdued face. I wanted to hear what Dan would say first. We drove while I waited. My memory of what he said is vague, but it turned down the fire in my heart-air balloon. He didn't seem to share my enthusiasm.

The whole idea of breaking free led me to think of my dear friend Naomi. Here was her chance to go back to San Luis Obispo. I called her to find out what she was thinking.

Naomi explained how her point of view changed. She was for staying put. Then she reminded me of when I told her that we should bloom where God planted us. It was not what I expected to hear. I thought for sure I would have a comrade for the great exodus.

Afterward, I brought my point of view to Dan. His wind wasn't blowing enough to fill my sails, much less be powerful enough to carry our ship to the free land. I pulled out the paddles. There was no way I was going to let this one go.

Soon after, Dan said he told Miguel what I had to say about the decision we were facing. He said that when Miguel heard how I felt, he laughed.

My heart sank. I contemplated what I would do if Dan wouldn't leave. My thoughts spun dizzy circles that twisted my sleep. *Could I refuse to go along with Dan? What would happen if I said I would not stay?* I imagined myself walking down the street past the others in their front yards. *How would they respond to me? What position would that put the children? How would it affect our marriage and family life?* I wanted to leave the covenant with a passion. However, I couldn't picture how it would play out. All I could do was pray that Dan would go.

160

We had a long, open talk about it. Dan had some serious concerns. He said, "If we leave the fellowship, we will still live on Candlewick. They would consider our kids outsiders. How would that work with their relationships with their friends?"

"You've got a point. Do you think the other kids will end up shunning ours or treat them differently?"

"I don't know, but I can't see how it wouldn't happen."

He's right about that.

He continued. "We can't afford a Christian school for the kids. We'd have to send them to public school."

"Well, I don't think that's such a terrible thing. We are to be in the world, just not of it. How can we be the salt of the earth if we are living just unto ourselves? If our children are in public school, we could touch others beyond Tamarisk. We could be more effective witnesses for the Lord."

"I don't see how it would work for us to leave. It's too complicated."

My frustration sizzled. Here was our chance to get out from underneath Tamarisk's rule. We had an opportunity to live like other Christians.

"It would probably be messy, but after the struggle, it would be worth it."

"I can't see it working out without us putting our house up for sale and moving away. I won't do that. We will remain right here."

"Does that mean we can't leave the church?"

"We are staying with Tamarisk."

I was butting my head up against an impenetrable wall. There was no winning this one. Dan was unwilling to face the tearing-away process we would have to go through. Without the guts to plow through the overwhelming opposition, my high hopes turned to tears.

CHAPTER 50

May I Be Excused?

Two families left the fellowship. I never saw them again. Life continued as it did before.

Miguel announced that the people who stayed with Tamarisk would be required to sign a written covenant. The leadership was drawing up the document. He said it would be up for review and signature at the approaching retreat. It was mandatory that everyone be in attendance.

Meanwhile, my father was having severe cardiovascular problems that were life-threatening if he didn't undergo coronary bypass surgery. They put him on a waiting list for an opening in the surgeon's schedule. When Papa called us to tell us what was going on, his words seemed laced with fear. He said he wanted me to be there.

Then came the terrible news. They set the date for a day when we would be up at the retreat.

I brought the situation up to Miguel, explaining my father's fear and need for support. When I asked if I could be excused from the meeting, Miguel's demeanor reflected concern for my father. Apologizing and sympathetic, he told me it would be the only time we could read and sign the document. It was imperative I be present. He assured me that the fellowship would join in prayer for my father's complete recovery.

I left that conversation tormented. I thought God was asking me to prove who I loved more, Jesus or my father. It was a terrible test for me because of what Jesus says in Matthew 10:34–39: "Do not think that I came to bring peace on earth. I did not come to bring peace but a sword. For I have come to set a man against his father, a daughter against her mother, and a daughter-in-law against mother-in-law; and a man's enemies will be of his own household. He who loves father or mother more than Me is not worthy of Me. And he who loves his son or daughter more than Me is not worthy of Me. And he who does not take his cross and follow after Me is not worthy of Me. He who finds his life will lose it, and he who loses his life for My sake will find it."

Rebelling didn't occur to me. I just took it as a stab in the heart. I wanted to be with my father. Our relationship broke when I was young. The Lord gave me a forgiving spirit toward him, and I longed to show my father that God loved him. It was a way of practicing what I had preached to him for years.

It was grueling to tell my father I wouldn't be with him for his operation. "I'm sorry, Papa. I won't be able to be there."

"Why not?"

"Our church is meeting to make a critical decision about what direction we will go from here."

"I don't understand what could be so important."

"I need to be there. The issue will have a profound effect on our family's future. I can't miss it."

"Well, if it means that much to you …"

"Papa, our whole church knows about your situation and will pray for you.

I promise that as soon as it is over, I'll come and see you."

It seemed like there was a gaping hole in my words. They landed in silence. My father's lack of response left me in anguish over having to disappoint him to obey Miguel. But it wasn't for me to question his leadership. Doing as he said was my way of showing my true love for my Heavenly Father.

Papa's surgery was a success. As soon as we arrived home, I repacked, put Matthew and the baby in the car, and then drove over the snowy mountain pass. We saw my father in the hospital. He looked roughed up, but he was doing well, thank God. I told him that our church was keeping him in their prayers. My choice to be with them instead of him was like an invisible lead in the room.

CHAPTER 51

The Child Swap

Miguel came up with another one of his big ideas. He said it was apparent to him that there was too much inconsistency with the way parents were handling the discipline of their children. Therefore, we would have a mandatory week-long child swap. He said it would bring to light those who were not handling their kids the way they should.

Oh Lord, what now? How's this one going to play out? I felt a familiar tightness in my core as he continued with his plan. Leadership would determine who would get whose kids.

Instant fear grabbed me. My heart pounded. *Where will our kids have to stay? What if they go to Jerry's, or Frank's, or one of the other elders?* I worried because they might scrutinize and treat them harshly. I knew how loose ended our young ones could sometimes be.

The Lord had mercy. They assigned them to Bob and Naomi. I was happy we could send them to fun, easygoing people.

Dan and I had Jackson and Annabelle's family of seven children, plus an older teenage girl, to help us. We had three more children than we were used to.

That wasn't all that was going on for me. The head teacher of the kindergarten hurt her back, incapacitating her. They called me to take Nadine's place for the rest of the year. It was an unfamiliar responsibility for me. My job was to take her reading and math students, plus oversee the other k- teachers. By God's grace, it was spring break, so I had an entire week to prepare to slide onto the base. It was a huge undertaking.

While the kids were at Naomi's, Luke came down with a severe ear infection. His ear was draining. Miguel said I couldn't bring him home to care for him, which was upsetting. However, I could be the one to take him to the ear, nose, and throat doctor.

My little Luke had to have his ear suctioned out to remove the infected fluid. He was frightened and crying throughout the procedure. It broke my heart to take him back to Naomi's instead of caring for him myself. The only consolation was that she was the one to take my place.

Because I had an infant, I had been a stay-home babysitter. I had to do a lot to be ready to teach again. I was preoccupied with getting my lesson plans put together, etc. My teenage helper took care of the children. She served meals, changed diapers, entertained the little ones, and kept tabs on them for me. Thank the Lord; I couldn't have made it through the week without that precious girl. It was tax season, so Dan was at the office until late in the evenings. He spent very little time with our young guests.

It seemed like the whole church sighed with relief when it was over. We all got our kids back after church on the last Sunday of Easter vacation. The next day, we all jumped back on the Tamarisk school exercise wheel.

CHAPTER 52

Perplexing Scrutiny

It baffled me they chose to have me be the head teacher in the kindergarten instead of my close friend Annie, who was already in place teaching reading and math. She had more experience than I did. I thought she was one of the most conscientious, dedicated, and loving teachers.

The principal of the school, Eleanor, and Marie-Anne came to me. They told me that Annie was going through discipline for being rebellious and lazy. They spoke of her as if she was way out of line. As head teacher, they wanted me to keep a very close eye on her, making sure she had thorough lesson plans, did all her tasks with a cheerful attitude, and was respectful of all the rules and my authority. If she was complacent in any of these areas, I was to report her immediately.

It shocked me. I couldn't understand what they told me. *Annie? What could she possibly have done to deserve such harsh scrutiny? No one I know works as hard as she does or is more dedicated to the children.*

I didn't want to be critical of her attitude or work. It was weird to me they would place me over her in such a way. I said that it surprised me and didn't recognize such qualities in her, but I agreed to keep an eye on her.

When Annie and I got together, her attitude was what I considered being overly subservient and fearful of what I would think. She presented me with neat, well-organized, and thorough lesson plans. It baffled me that she worried that they weren't good enough. I let her know I thought they great and tried to put her at ease. Something seemed out of place. I found it disturbing.

Just as in the past, it delighted me to be in the classroom with Annie. She was like a right-hand lady for me, always anticipating ways she could help. I didn't enjoy being in a position of authority over her. It should have been the other way around. She knew more about the program than I did, yet she was always afraid of making a mistake. I was continuously trying to put her at ease. It wasn't right she should have to be fearful of what I thought.

Eleanor approached me to check up on her as if I would have something negative to say. I reassured her all was well and that Annie was an excellent worker with a proper attitude toward the children and me.

Annie was in her second trimester of pregnancy and still having a terrible struggle with nausea and vomiting. She couldn't keep water down. My heart tore for her. Leadership would not let her take time off. She seemed stressed out, beaten down, and overboard with anxiety.

One day before school, Annie collapsed in front of Max and Candy's house. Me and a few others, including Mary-Anne, helped her onto Candy's sofa. She was crying and shaking. She needed to see her doctor. However, Mary-Anne ignored me when I said so.

Marie-Anne took over the scene. She bent down next to Annie and spoke to her. Her tone sounded empathetic. She told her she understood that it was hard, but she needed to accept and embrace what the Lord was trying to say to her.

What? Can't she see that Annie is under too much pressure, is sick, and desperately needs to take some time off? This can't be good for her baby. What does Mary-Anne mean by "embrace the situation?" What is she talking about? I could tell that there was more going on than I could see. No matter what I thought, it wasn't for me to question an elder's wife. It was evident leadership knew something was going on that I didn't.

All I could do was to step up my prayers for Annie. I implored God to have them give her time off. I prayed for the Lord's protection over her baby.

Annie went to the doctor. Marilee told her she was getting dehydrated, and if she continued to be unable to hold water down, she would hospitalize her. Leadership's response was to let her have the rest of the week off. They made her be back in school the following Monday. All this made no sense to me.

Even though Annie was so sick, I never heard her complain against them. She seemed hypervigilant and terrified to say anything negative about the way leadership was treating her.

It showed me how hard and picky our leaders could be and how dangerous things could get if they somehow perceived a negative attitude or a lack of conscientiousness. It also showed me how little our lives meant considering the success of our school.

CHAPTER 53

A Crack in the Window

Summer came. As usual, we camped with the fellowship at Bodega Bay. About a week after we unpacked, Dan and I gathered our six kids and beach gear for our annual trip to Tahoe. When we got home, it was time for all the planning and prep for another school year.

Taking care of the details was complicated. There had to be teachers to cover each subject for all the kindergarten through high school subjects. Teachers needed babysitters for their preschool children, and everyone had to have a ride to and from school. We had our uniform swap in time to make necessary purchases. They ordered the books, and then the dads had to cover them with brown paper. Then there was shopping for and labeling a myriad of supplies.

After we got our teaching assignments, we made our preparations and met to orient the fathers. Classrooms were set up and decorated. The operation took up at least half the time school wasn't in session.

❧

Shortly after school started, we all went on our twenty-one-day "Daniel fast" again. Candy was facing her baby's due date, but leadership was hard-nosed about it. She had to eat vegetables legumes along with the rest of us. I wondered how she would make it without collapsing or something.

When we were in the last part of the fast, Candy was getting weak. Her husband, Max, approached leadership and asked if she could break the fast early. Leadership denied his request. I couldn't fathom why they treated her that way.

Before the fast ended, she began labor. Max put his foot down. Against the mandate, he told her to break it.

Shock vibrated the fellowship. Some women expressed relief for her, and others seemed offended. Max's audacity astounded me. Deep down, I admired him for taking charge of the situation.

I wonder to this day what Miguel said about it. All I picked up was an eerie silence.

Every year I was given more responsibilities. This year, I also taught second-grade math and was frequently used as a substitute teacher for the afternoon classes. I still taught reading and math in kindergarten. As head teacher, it was my responsibility to make sure lesson plans came in monthly, and everything ran as it should. I was laid back about it. I knew these women were knowledgeable and faithful about their jobs.

As time passed, I felt more and more respected by the school administration and accepted by Miguel. He gave me a white lace head covering. I considered that to be a gesture of approval, which warmed my heart toward him.

I came to a place where I accepted being extremely busy. It was hard work to take care of my family and do my best for the school. The older children did more to care for themselves and help with the younger ones. Matthew took little John from his car seat and then handed him over to the babysitter. He used to sit with him reading storybooks. Sweet memories.

I worked alongside some diamond quality women. Together, we laid down a lot of miles, tasted many tears, loved, fought, forgave, and belly laughed. As far as the eye could see, we knew one another well.

Miguel spent long chunks of time out of town. When he was gone, Frank stood over us. Frank was mellow in comparison. When he was in charge, breathing was easier.

After one of his retreats, it seemed that something inside Miguel had melted. His sharp demeanor seemed to have its edge filed down. He leaned on the podium and gave a message he titled "Pillow Talk." He spoke about talking things out with your spouse. He expressed himself gently and thoughtfully. It was weird.

In March, I was pregnant again. It delighted Dan and me. However, the haunting fear of miscarrying cast its shadow over me. I had learned that having a baby in my womb didn't mean I would hold one at my breast. Dan seemed far more confident than I was, an encouragement that eased some of my worries.

I remember mornings, sitting with my students, trying to swallow nausea that pressed against my tonsils as I reviewed their word cards with them. I hated being morning sick, yet it was a sign that the pregnancy was progressing as it should. It made me ill and comforted me at the same time.

My mood rose from what it had once been. The binding that chafed my spirit seemed to loosen. The struggle of fighting against my perimeter lost its momentum. Though I had accepted our circumstances, Annie and I had a standing joke about how fast we would leave if we could.

"Look at her go. Her hair's on fire!"

We would laugh, saying, "Don't choke on the smoke people—we're out of here!"

Acceptance and humor aside, we still made frequent comments about stress. We would go over our to-do lists and talk about having to bring our school bags along with us to catch every free minute to do our homework. It was nuts.

I often complained to Dan about how I felt like I couldn't go on like this. My mother voiced her concern for me. She said I was carrying too much of a load and that it wasn't healthy. Though her words rang true in me, I wouldn't allow myself the luxury of heeding her advice.

Something had to give, or I would drop on my face or lose my mind. I worried that my uptightness would put me at risk of losing my baby. Dan listened to me, but what could he say? "Don't worry. It doesn't do either of you any good."

Our friends Jackson and Annabelle had more children than we did. They also had the resources to hire a nanny to help. She went in the morning and stayed until the evening. I drooled at the thought.

Dan saw my need for a break from somewhere. Annabelle's nanny came from a family of immigrants from Ukraine. She had a sister who was looking for work. We couldn't pay to have her work as many hours, but she was happy with what we could offer. Elsa was an extra pair of eyes. She watched over the children and helped with the house. Her presence was a gift from God.

CHAPTER 54

The Scent of Rebellion

The wet and chill of the winter months transformed into warmer, breezy days. Trees blossomed, bulbs burst into colorful flowers, and tax season was finally over. Marilee said that my baby's heart was beating as it should. The end of the school year was in sight, meaning relief was just around the corner. Things were sunny-side up for me.

Spring fever drew me out of the house. I wandered down the street, watching the neighborhood kids play ball and ride their bikes, until I saw Candy in her front yard. After we chatted a few minutes, she invited me in.

Candy was someone I admired. I met her when she was leading a women's Bible study in the years before the Blessed Spirit. She always had an intense desire to know Jesus and be pleasing to Him. We'd been through the ups, downs, and curves of a long road together.

We went into her bedroom, where we could talk without children breaking up our conversation. She shared what was burdening her. It honored me because she seemed to feel safe with me. I sat listening. She was caught struggling over being stuck in the confines of Tamarisk and longed to be able to do things there was no time for. She wanted to be able to play tennis and get involved with the community outside our church.

Her voice carried frustration and had an angry beat pushing it forward. Her words vibrated with the same feelings I had worked hard to overcome. I was well acquainted with a heart that wanted to break free. It was a dangerous place to be. There was no happiness or peace in it.

After all that I went through in the years prior, I finally had some peace. In my mind, Tamarisk was where the Lord wanted me. I had to find laughter and joy in my days or waste away in misery.

As Candy spoke, dread and turmoil rose in my gut. I didn't want to hear her talking like that. I thought she was bordering on rebellion. My mind flashed back to the enthusiasm she had when we were first getting involved. *I followed her into this, and now she wants freedom.*

"Yes, I know how you feel, Candy. I've been there. God has carried me through the same thing. I've repented and embraced that this is where He wants me, and I feel much better about it now."

She seemed resistant to my words. I could tell I wasn't going to talk her out of her frame of mind, though I wondered if the Lord wanted me to confront her insubordinate attitude the way others had done to me. I cowered, not wanting to be that way to my old friend.

I steeped in what Candy shared with me. It worried me. I thought she was in the wrong place spiritually. According to all I had learned, the Lord did not want such an attitude tolerated.

After contemplating how to handle the situation, I saw Miguel watching the kids clean up when school was over for the day. I knew he would want to be aware of discontentment in the ranks. Though I felt terrible betraying my old friend, in my mind, I thought it would be wrong if I didn't inform him.

Without giving him any details, I told him I picked up on a rebellious attitude brewing in Candy. He seemed uplifted that I was sharing my observation with him. Miguel patted me on the shoulder, thanked me, and told me, "You're my little canary."

It made me feel special.

CHAPTER 55

Audacity

Miguel's tight grip was loosening. It seemed the word "mandatory" was softening under the influence of the retreats he was taking. With him out of town, the atmosphere was lighter. When he announced that this year, the Bodega Bay camping trip would be an optional church activity, my spirit soared. The last thing I felt like doing was to drag my tired, swelling body through chores in the damp sand.

I didn't bother asking Dan if I could stay home. I flat out told him I wasn't going. He didn't seem pleased with my insistence, but what could he say? Dan was a kindhearted man. He said he would take the children so I could have a break at home. *Ahh, perfect vacation!*

The school year was behind us. However, it wouldn't be long before it was time to prepare for the following term. I wondered what that would be like for our family. If this baby lived, we would have seven children. I tried to have faith that God could provide me with all that I would need to continue with the school effort. In Matthew 19:26, Jesus said, "With men, it is impossible, but with God, all things are possible." Still, I couldn't fathom how He would work it out.

Then Candy's husband, Max, took a stand on behalf of his wife and family. He announced that Candy would not continue to work in the school. He said it was too much of a burden for her.

I was astounded. I could hardly grasp Max's audacity. However, I honored him for being willing to take the inevitable heat. He would have to face leadership and the angry people in the fellowship. Though he was bucking the system, in a hidden crevice in my heart, I was behind him.

We needed all the help we could get to keep the school running. Losing a teacher and babysitter was a threat to all the mothers left carrying the load. We were so stretched as it was. How could we keep the school running at full speed?

My antennas raised, and intrigue took over. I could sense the rumble vibrating through the fellowship. Some folks were quiet, while it offended others. How could Max pull Candy out of circulation when we were all having a hard time keeping up?

The time came for our family's Tahoe vacation. We would be out of the epicenter of the earthquake. It was going to be interesting to go home to the aftershocks.

I finally had come to a place of believing that I was entering the narrow gate. My compliant attitude made me feel that my baby was on safer ground. The absence of turmoil gave me energy and some peace. However, the truth of my heart woke in me when Max stood up on behalf of his wife.

No matter what I had been telling myself, my need for a break was overwhelming. I couldn't help but want Max's motion to effect a change in our situation. I longed for Dan to recognize how things were pushing me into the impossible. *Please, Dan, can't you see that it's too much for me also?*

We headed to the lake. As Dan drove, I complained about how my stamina was waning. Near a breaking point, my level of stress affected my ability to handle all the issues that came up with the kids.

"Every time I turn around, I find myself on edge and impatient over insignificant things."

"Yes, I know it's hard."

"Something has to give. I can't keep going like this."

"Um-hum." Dan kept his eyes on the road.

It seemed like he heard me but didn't grasp the intensity of my words. With a familiar frustration of wishing he had more to say, I let go and sat back in silence. Tears blurred my vision as I looked out my window so he couldn't see my face.

Am I falling back into being rebellious and angry? Will it hurt the baby if I entertain such thoughts? Is it wrong for me to want freedom from so much responsibility? An anxiety spasm twisted my spirit. *Oh dear God, help me to keep my mind in the right place.*

"For the weapons of our warfare are not carnal but mighty in God for pulling down strongholds, casting down arguments and every high thing that exalts itself against the knowledge of God, bringing every thought captive to the obedience of Christ" (2 Corinthians 10:4–5 [NKJV]). *How can I know where God wants my mind to be?*

We spent our time in Tahoe at the beach and hiking during the days. Dan seemed relaxed and enjoying our time away from home. I was glad to be back where I grew up and relished baking my pregnant body in the warm Tahoe sun. However, I couldn't relax and stay focused while I tried to read my book.

My swirling emotions wouldn't stay confined to the parameters of compliant thoughts. I couldn't stop thinking of how Max stood up for Candy. He was protecting his wife. I envied her.

I felt I was breaking into Dan's peace of mind every time I brought the subject of my stress up to him. He appeared to listen but had little to say. It seemed he wouldn't go as far as Max did. It bewildered and hurt me.

The more I wanted a change in the system, the more guilt shrouded me like a cold, wet cloak. During the nights, when all was quiet, a battle was at full swing in my spirit. Fear that my desire was rebellious ricocheted off the walls of my heart. Anxiety smoldered in my stomach.

While Dan slept, I wrapped my arms around my belly. *Please, God, keep my baby alive. Don't let this torment suck the life out of this little one. Forgive me, Jesus, if I'm out of line, but I can't help but feel things need to be different. How can I find Your peace?*

CHAPTER 56

The Dream

The only way we could continue with the school was to cut back on the grades we covered. That would leave parents having to find other schools for their children. Few families could afford private Christian school. We would have to enroll our children in the disdained public school system. It would expose our children to "the world," something the ranks would buck against.

I welcomed the idea. Through the years, my opinion changed. Our focus stayed on ourselves as a church. Other than our ministry to mothers from the crisis line, we did very little outreach to the community. If we mingled in the public schools, we could be more effective witnesses. "You are the light of the world. A city that is set on a hill cannot be hidden. Nor do they light a lamp and put it under a basket, but on a lampstand, and it gives light to all who are in the house. Let your light so shine before men, that they may see your good works and glorify your Father in heaven" (Matthew 5:14–16 [NKJV]).

I gave all my arguments to Dan. He never disagreed with me and seemed to comprehend my logic, but he wouldn't jump onto my bandwagon. It's as if he just stood there watching me fume. He seemed more wrapped up enjoying our time away with the kids.

In the middle of one night, toward the end of our vacation, I had a vivid dream. In it, I saw a large multicolored map of the United States. Then, a hand holding a sledgehammer appeared. It raised and then slammed down on the Sacramento Valley. When it hit, particles from beneath its head scattered in all directions, landing on different parts of the states across the country. I woke and sat up with a gasp. I felt relief. Hope poured like warm oil over my frustration. *Is God trying to tell me something? Could it be that the Lord will come down on Tamarisk Covenant Fellowship and scatter us? Will the ones that break apart get dispersed to other parts of the country? Oh, if that could only be true. Change, Hallelujah!*

CHAPTER 57

Meeting Adjourned

Hope escaped from its prison cell. However, I continued to question where it came from—God or me. I could see the dream over again when I closed my eyes.

I worried that I was rebellious. Deep down, I wanted to see the church broken apart. *If I'm rebellious, will God take my baby?* My stomach would twist and burn when the thought came to mind. I would lay awake in the night with hope and fear playing racquetball with my emotions. The baby's movements consoled me that at present. Everything was OK. They soothed my spirit like listening to a sweet lullaby.

We came home from our vacation to unrest about what would happen with the school. Max stood his ground. We had to proceed without Candy. The school administration set a time to meet with everyone involved. It was to discuss how we would put things together without her.

Miguel said that it was never mandatory to have a school. He said we had to figure out what we wanted to put into it. It surprised me to hear that because my experience said something different. However, there was no way I would argue about it.

It was great news to me.

I figured that since it was our decision, I was done. However, no matter how much I tried to convince Dan, he didn't back me up. He listened but would not say I could pull out. To my hot frustration, he was quiet.

The school administration set up a meeting to discuss how we would continue without Candy. When I pressed Dan to let me out, he said, "Let's wait until we find out what everyone else will do."

"Why wait?"

"I want to hear what other people are saying."

"Who cares? I cannot continue the way I have been. It's too much for me to handle."

"We will see what happens."

It exasperated me. I could not understand why Dan seemed to be dragging his feet. To me, it was apparent that I should quit.

"Where will our kids go to school?" he asked.

"We can't afford a private Christian school."

"They will have to go to the public schools in our area. Maybe that's why this whole thing is happening. It could be God wants us to reach out to the world."

He was quiet.

At the meeting, everyone sat in a circle. Miguel and Sandi were conspicuously absent. They left it up to the fathers and teachers to handle. A subdued rankling permeated the atmosphere.

There was a discussion about the cutbacks needed to keep the school running. It was clear that the older grades would not be workable to maintain. To get feedback, they went around the room so that everyone could speak their minds.

Some people seemed deeply troubled. They were determined to keep the school running. To my delight, others wanted to pull their support from the effort. As they shared their thoughts, I could barely sit still. I kept nudging Dan, who kept to himself.

Our turn to speak came last. I trembled and took a firm hold of Dan's arm. "Come on, Dan, let me out," I whispered.

"We will not continue with the school," he announced.

Victory! Hallelujah! Praise God, and thank You, Jesus! I could have danced.

They set another time to discuss continuing the school. We adjourned.

We gathered our things and left the room. Some people seemed shocked, angry, and fearful. The rest of us had subdued smiles and seemed content with how things turned out.

Walking down the corridor on the way to the parking lot, I relished knowing they wouldn't involve me in planning for the fall. The weight of the school dissipated. I floated home.

CHAPTER 58

Exposure

Tamarisk school was in a tizzy. They had to assess who they had left to work with and figure out what they could still be able to teach. Not my problem. It didn't bother me that I was part of their undoing. I thought it was a move of the Holy Spirit.

Infiltrating the public school system with a Christian influence enthused me. *Dan and I can join the PTA. When I get acclimated and have more energy, I can help the teachers in their classrooms. I will still be involved with the children's education.*

We didn't have the Tamarisk school meeting until the first day the public schools began. We were two days behind in starting school. I, with my baby bump, drove to three different places to admit my kids into their new schools.

I was very embarrassed that I was enrolling my kids late. I felt odd and out of place, like a hillbilly walking into a big city bank.

The secretary asked questions. "What school did they go to before?"

"Tamarisk Christian School."

She looked puzzled. "Where is that located?"

"It was a cooperative homeschool run by our church. We leased a wing at the community center."

Her eyebrows raised.

"Well, do you have their transcripts?"

"Yes." *Thank you, Jesus, they kept the proper records.*

The office in the elementary school had several ladies just standing around talking to one another. It seemed like they were eyeing me. The secretary gave me a thick stack of papers to read, fill out, and sign by the following day.

I said goodbye to the kids and released them into the care of those I had worked so hard to keep them from. The years and exhaustion had transformed my thinking.

When I picked the kids up in the afternoon, they seemed to take the change in stride. As far as I could see from their behavior, they were upbeat about this major turn of events. In my mind, our family was embarking on a huge adventure.

Tamarisk's atmosphere was changing. It felt like taking off a tight girdle. Miguel continued to spend most of his time away. Without everyone's concentration focused on the school, there was more time for thought and general questioning of where God was leading us as a church.

Miguel's most recent messages portrayed openness for feedback about what was on people's minds. I had a deep stirring about what we had been through, resulting from Miguel's influence over the years. With the extra time I had, I sat down at my keyboard and started a letter to share what I was feeling with Miguel.

When I opened the letter, I had a tenderness toward a man who seemed to be transforming from a hardheaded leader to someone who was being softened by the Holy Spirit. I felt compassion and mercy for him, though I thought it was important that he see the ways our family had bruised while under his covering. I spent a month weeping to him through my fingertips.

Meanwhile, what had been a subliminal, angry rumble emerged from under the covers of daily life in the fellowship. I wasn't the only one who was hurting from things that had happened. Though I felt rebellious, I listened as other women dared to put hidden puzzle pieces on the table. They shared events and feelings they were told or had been afraid to discuss.

I can't do justice to the painful stories. Miguel, the elders, and their wives implicated people of sins they didn't commit. I could remember covenant meetings when they were on the hot seat for things like trying to seduce Miguel and the other elders. They accused some of rebellion or having a Jezebel spirit. I learned the truth about how they came to be blacklisted. No wonder some had become thin as rails, withdrawn, and depressed.

The fog that had accumulated on my lenses cleared away. Mysteries began to make perfect sense. Because other members spoke up, layers of guilt for talking behind Miguel's back lifted. I could see with no doubt that he had a perverted mind and promoted lies to manipulate and oppress God's people.

By the time I finished my letter, I thought of Miguel as a wolf in sheep's clothing. I vaguely remembered passages in the Bible. "Beware of false prophets, who come to you in sheeps clothing, but inwardly are ravenous wolves. You will know them by their fruits. Do men gather grapes from thornbushes or figs from thistles?" (Matthew 7:15–16 [NKJV]) "For I know this, that after my departure savage wolves will come in among you, not sparing the flock. Also from among yourselves men will rise up, speaking perverse things, to draw away disciples after themselves" (Acts 20:29–30 [NKJV]).

I shared my revelation with Dan. He listened attentively and affirmed there were things wrong with the way Miguel used his authority. However, he wasn't forthcoming with much of what he thought. I felt like I was having to convince him the situation was menacing enough to leave the church without fear that we would act against God's will.

One man in the fellowship found a book about cults. It passed hand to hand to some members of the fellowship. Soon, there was an angry buzz and a suggestion that Tamarisk Covenant Fellowship was one of them.

It split the church in two. Everyone seemed to acknowledge there were things wrong with our fellowship, but not everyone was looking at it as a cult. Some people clung to the validity of the covenant as God-ordained.

Miguel disappeared. There was no way for anyone to face him with grievances. Frank, the elder who was left in charge, had to face the tumult and confusion.

CHAPTER 59

A Line in the Sand

Thanksgiving was less than two weeks away. Frank broke the leadership's silence. He announced that Miguel would be returning for the Sunday service following the holiday. During that meeting, Miguel would address the fellowship and be open to our questions and concerns.

Tittering buzzed over the phone lines and conversations swirled among people. I have no clue what those clinging to the covenant were saying among themselves, but I know those members well enough to surmise they were well into communication.

Dan and I shared things various members had told us. Miguel was the mastermind, and the elders were his minions behind countless manipulative scenarios that hurt adults and children in a myriad of ways. Dan and I were awestricken.

I remember one time Dan and I were talking about it while washing the dishes.

"I can't see any reason to stay. I want to leave," I implored.

"Miguel has changed. Maybe he is repentant."

"I don't care if he's changed. I don't want him to be our pastor."

"Where would we go? What would happen to the kids? We'd still live here."

"I'm sure we can figure that out. They're in public school already."

"I'm going to wait so I can hear what Miguel has to say. Also, it is important to know what everyone's got on their mind. I want to hear people out before I decide."

From being married to him for fifteen years, I knew it was time to resign myself from all forms of persuasion.

Dan and I took our clan to Reno for Thanksgiving with Papa. It was a treat this time because we were spending the nights at a nice hotel. We used to stay at my father's house, but it was getting harder to deal with so many kids among his porcelain treasures. It was nice not to have to watch my stepmother wiping their fingerprints off the surfaces.

The baby was due around December 5, so I was on the watch for labor contractions. It was a bit of a risk being so far away from home, but Dan was in a forge-forward mode. That Thanksgiving, I was filled with the anticipation of having the baby and what would happen at the meeting. I wondered which event would happen first.

My mind was stuck on everything that was going on with our church. I held myself back from talking about it because I was afraid Dan would get irritated with me. The thoughts running through my head were heavy duty.

What if Dan decides to stay with the fellowship? How will I manage the situation? There's no way I'm staying with this church. If Dan won't leave, I will have to divide our home. Daddy does and Mommy doesn't. A strong sense of resolve was like a tree inside me. I knew the wind could blow hard, but it would remain standing.

CHAPTER 60

Burn, Baby, Burn

We left my father's house on Saturday so we would be home for the meeting with Miguel come Sunday morning. Once again, we were leaving Papa behind because our church was calling.

Sunday morning came. There are things about it I can remember almost as if it just happened. It was a bright, crisp November day. I was excited and curious about what Miguel had to say. I felt like a wild horse prancing around the confines of a coral. Dan was calm and didn't have much to say. The kids seemed oblivious to the intensity of the day.

As far as it concerned me, I was leaving the church. I had no fear that it would interfere with our marriage. It would only mean that we would attend different churches. *But what about the children?* That was something that I would have to work out later. *By that time, Dan will give up and leave. He will never tolerate such a split in our home.*

Miguel wasn't in the sanctuary while everyone was taking their seats. Everyone seemed pensive, and the atmosphere had a subliminal animosity. I felt like there were two basic camps— the forgiving and the wrathful.

We expected to see Miguel's pastor from Los Angeles at the meeting. Word had it he was coming to mediate the situation. Instead, a man I had never seen before accompanied him. They took their seats in the front pew.

I believe it was Frank who stood at the podium. He spoke briefly and then opened the mike to Miguel. He gave a vague confession of making mistakes and being too hard on us. The details escaped me. However, I remember thinking his confession was too general. It didn't seem to hit the nails on the head. His expression of remorse came off as flat to me. *He's just going through the motions.*

Frank opened the floor for people to address Miguel individually. At first, everyone spoke respectfully, though some had fire in their eyes. Most of the grievances brought up were regarding the church finances. We were required to give 15 percent of our gross income to the church. People wanted to know where the money went.

Some people spoke about forgiveness and being merciful to Miguel for wrongs suffered. They said we could all grow from this.

The forgiveness issue has nothing to do with whether I stay. No way am I sticking around.

The intensity increased as the subject of coercion came around. Miguel was quiet. His accomplice got up and spoke for a short time. The only thing that he said that echoes in my mind is "No one put a gun to your head."

Eyes rolled over that statement.

Before the meeting closed, Miguel and the man left the sanctuary. It seemed that Miguel's accomplice was there to defend and protect him.

I was glad when the meeting was over. When we stepped outside, the sky was crystal blue with billowing white clouds. I was content in my resolve. *I never have to come here again. Miguel will not rule over me anymore.*

I lifted my face toward the sun and felt the breeze blowing through my hair.

As people were still coming out of the sanctuary, Frank came out in front of the church holding the covenant document, with all our original signatures. After clearing a space around him, he set it on the concrete walkway.

What's he doing?

He lit it on fire.

"Dan, look." I grabbed onto him and pointed at the papers on the ground.

For a few glorious minutes, I watched as the flames licked the pages that bound us together for the rest of our lives. I saw them turn to ash. *Oh my god, I can't believe how wonderful this is!*

Dan's muscles relaxed as he breathed, "Hallelujah, It's over."

I could have danced. I kept saying, "We're free, Dan! We're free!"

We gathered our children, climbed into our van and drove home to our new life out from under the Tamarisk tree.

EPILOGUE

2020

Five days later, our lively little Mary was born.

After our departure, I read everything I could find about abusive churches and cults. I was trying to piece together what happened to us and find a way to get straightened out. I believed we would just flow into normal life. I was wrong. Our whole family was traumatized.

It didn't take long to realize we were in serious trouble. I talked to my dear doctor, Marilee, to see if she knew of any ethical counselors. She referred us to one. I asked a friend who had left the fellowship many years prior if she knew of some with a good reputation. It was the same person, so we figured he was probably worthy of whatever trust we had left.

He turned out to be like an angel sent by God. At our first session, he told us we should always listen to our gut and follow our hearts. That day, he asked us if we had ever heard about setting boundaries. *Boundaries are good?* To this day, I'm profoundly grateful I followed my floundering instincts.

Going to church did not work. It left me confused. The pastors spoke from the same Bible and preached many of the same things I had heard throughout the Tamarisk years. It was like floating around in a galaxy of questions. If it wasn't the real Jesus I had laid my life down for, then *who is He? How could all this have happened?* Deep in my heart, I knew God would never betray me. Everything was a disastrous mistake.

Something in the depths of my spirit still believed the Bible was true, but it left me perplexed. I was too overwhelmed and burned out to try to untie the knot. However, even though it collected dust, it stayed at my bedside. I could not let go of it.

After a year of counseling, I started to open my Bible again. I began by reading the Psalms and found them to be an antibiotic for my infected spiritual wounds. Then I ventured into Proverbs. To this day, I try to read a chapter of each book every morning before I start my day.

It has been a long process of psychotherapy and examining the Bible, to straighten out the twists and kinks Miguel's crafty lies did to my mind. I see how my sincere faith was contorted so I could be led astray.

Now I can understand a myriad of ways I went wrong and did not walk in the truth. To begin with, I did not know enough of what the Bible says about those who are our spiritual leaders. "Shepherd, the flock of God, which is among you, serving as overseers, not by compulsion but willingly, not for dishonest gain but eagerly; nor as lords over those entrusted to you, but being examples to the flock" (1Peter 5:2–3 [NKJV]). Jesus said, "You know that the rulers of the Gentiles lord it over them, and those who are great exercise authority over them. Yet it shall not be so among you; but whoever wishes to be great among you, let him be your servant" (Matthew 20:25–26 [NKJV]). These verses don't say that a shepherd (pastor) is to be a commander. Miguel was not walking according to scripture.

It's okay to question someone who professes to be a spiritual leader. "Beloved, do not believe every spirit, but test the spirits, whether they are from God; because many false prophets have gone out into the world" (1 John 4:1 [NKJV]). So much for blind obedience.

After many years of working with licensed Christian counselors and a child psychologist, we have been able to comb the tangles from our family's storm-tossed hair.

It's been agonizing to realize how I abused God's trust in me as a mother and unknowingly betrayed my precious children's faith in Jesus. He said, "If anyone causes one of these little ones—those who believe in Me, to stumble, it would be better for them to have a large millstone hung around their neck and be thrown into the depths of the sea" (Matthew 18:6 [NIV]).

All I could do is fall at Jesus's feet and beg His forgiveness and cleansing. The Bible says, "If we confess our sins, He is faithful and just to forgive us from all unrighteousness" (1 John 1: 9 [NKJV]). I have turned to my children and asked them if they can find it in their hearts to forgive me. It has taken me years of weeping to come to a place where I can begin to forgive myself.

I have clung to God's promise to heal our family. "If My people who are called by My name will humble themselves and pray and seek My face, and turn from their wicked ways, then I will hear from heaven, and will forgive their sin and heal their land" (2 Chronicles 7:14 [NKJV]). I thank God for His faithfulness.

My heart goes out to the people who had their lives torn apart while walking in the shadow of the Tamarisk tree. I have grieved for the children who were hurt. My prayer is that each one of them will find the Way, the Truth, and the Life.

Over twenty years after we were set free, a friend introduced us to his pastor. Both Dan and I had a good gut feeling about him. It was comforting to be around him, so we visited his church several times. Through his messages and interacting with the people, I have tasted God's warm milk and honey again. It has been like finding our way back home.